KT-173-906

82

David St. Clair (signature)

The Old Coach House
Thornton-le-Street
Thirsk
North Yorkshire YO7 4DS

Tel. Thirsk (0845) 522289

QUARTO   B.S.   ST. ANDREWS   SEP 1992

40p-

My Life and Game

Bjorn Borg

My Life and Game

as told to Gene Scott

Sidgwick & Jackson
London

First published in Great Britain in 1980
by Sidgwick and Jackson Limited

Copyright © 1980 Network Services SA

Filmset in 'Monophoto' Ehrhardt by
Servis Filmsetting Limited, Manchester

ISBN 0 283 98663 8

Printed in Great Britain by
William Clowes (Beccles) Limited
Beccles and London
for Sidgwick & Jackson Limited
1 Tavistock Chambers, Bloomsbury Way
London WC1A 2SG

B. BOR
9.

WITHDRAWN FROM LIBRARY

Contents

For Lennart,
for my mother and my father,
and for Mariana

Introduction by Gene Scott:

'The Right Stuff'

'You'd better do a lot with your approach when you play Borgie, because he's the world's best counter-puncher. Others may be flashier, McEnroe or Connors for instance, but Bjorn does more with the ball – more often – than anyone else in the game's history.'
Vitas Gerulaitis.

To collaborate in the writing of the definitive account of the life, technique, and tennis philosophy of the world's number one tennis player when the subject is only twenty-four may be over-ambitious. Many of Bjorn Borg's ideas and accomplishments are in the elusive process of maturing. For example, to Bjorn's feelings about his mother and father and Mariana will be added a dozen further layers in his life time, and certainly his tennis records at this point can only be an introduction to the eventual story. Still, Borg at twenty-four has already carved out a major niche among the greatest figures sport has ever seen, and the strong traits that have made him what he is are of intense interest to the entire tennis world right now.

More than several people were responsible for the chemistry that produced my collaboration with Bjorn Borg. Bob Kain, of the International Management Group (Borg's corporate agent), was steadfast and enthusiastic; Peter Schwed, my editor at Simon and Schuster, who had complete faith in Borg and more faith in me than merely admiring my backhand lob volley; my British publishers, Sidgwick & Jackson, who went all out for me; Margaret Sullivan, who typed the manuscript and corrected more than one inconsistency, was encouraging and committed to the task with a tough deadline to meet; Mariana Simionescu, Borg's fiancée, who cooked many an extra chop or hamburger so I could spend that extra hour with Bjorn; Lennart Bergelin, Borg's coach, who is so dedicated that he fretted lest I might interrupt his charge's training, but soon learned I was as attentive to Borg's need for space as he; and finally to Borg, the most loyal and sensitive athlete I know, who remembered that I looked after him when he played his first men's tournament in the United States nine years ago and believed I would still look after him.

What is 'Bjorn Borg'? Underneath the iceberg, who is he? Most of what the world knows of Borg comes straight from the press. He has few intimate friends on the tennis circuit though he is universally well liked. He is quiet and reserved, but no more so than fifty per cent of the rest of the touring professionals. Borg's personality, however, is probed with a laser's intensity because he is so completely his sport's number one.

Bjorn's shyness is magnified because his native tongue is Swedish while English is the official language of every tennis press conference – even in Sweden. Borg's answers are short and to the point, and he does not philosophize or offer more than the answer to the question asked. This is true of most of us who try to speak a second language. How nimble do you think an American or British TV commentator or journalist would be if you asked one of them the weather in Swedish?

By far the heaviest volume of tennis writing originates from America, Britain, and Australia, whose people are spoiled by not having to learn another language. At fifteen, Bjorn left school but still picked up a creditable facility in English. If he seems clipped and cold in his comments to the press, it is partly because of language, and partly because he became the youngest male champion in the sport's history, and yet has always been expected to respond with the clarity and depth of older tennis heroes.

Make no mistake, Borg has brains. Measure this man by his performance, perseverance or patience, or by his loyalty, or by his courage in crisis, and not by the measure of glibness. The press has trouble getting Borg's short answers straight. For instance, it is still reported that his pulse rate is 35. Nonsense. The myth dates back to when, at the age of eighteen, he took a medical exam for military service and was recorded as 38. It is now about 50 when he wakes up and around 60 in the afternoon. It can get higher at the peak of a match, of course. That may surprise reporters who assume Borg is ice-calm because brine flows in his veins.

Throughout this book the words and ideas are completely Borg's. I have occasionally interjected a few words where they seemed appropriate simply because Borg couldn't easily or modestly comment himself about a particular situation, but this is not a book about Bjorn Borg. It's a book by Bjorn Borg.

Tom Wolfe's best seller *The Right Stuff* penetrates the extraordinary fraternity of space age test pilots, whose guts and grace mean nothing without each other. Wolfe particularly eulogizes Chuck Yaegar, the world's first man to break the sound barrier in 1947. Wolfe describes Yaeger's moment of triumph, 'He was going faster than any man in history. It was almost silent up there. He was a master of the sky. His was a King's solitude unique and inviolate, above the dome of the world.'

That could have described Borg's elation after his fourth Wimbledon triumph – the identical isolation and glory. But victory is not enough to attain the elusive Olympus for either a Wimbledon champion or a fire-hot pilot. The quality of the man counts for as much as his heroic deed. Borg is made of the Right Stuff.

1. Borg on Borg

'Even if Borg weren't in the top ten, I'd admire him more than any other player. He never gives any trouble to the umps'.'
Anthony Levinson, nine years old, court side aide at the $300,000 Challenge Cup, Montreal, December 1979

I don't talk about myself much – unless you count telling reporters what the turning point against Connors was, or telling writers that I played well or didn't play so well against McEnroe. I don't volunteer much to reporters. If they ask me a question, I answer it briefly, but most of their questions are impersonal or foolish, or both. They watch my matches, why do they ask me what happened?

A good journalist knows as much about my strategy after a five-setter against Vitas Gerulaitis as I do. That is, if he cares as much about his profession as I do about mine. In fact, if a sports writer charts the points, he'll know more about my strengths and weaknesses in that particular battle than I would – until I see for myself the stat sheets on double faults, aces, winning volleys, and so forth.

Most of the material written about me has come as a result of that crazy institution known as the post match press conference. The session, in theory, makes sense. If every writer spent just twenty minutes with me after each match, I wouldn't have the time to play my next round. There are roughly sixty reporters in an early day post match press meeting at the US Open or Wimbledon, rising to 150 after the finals. So it would take between twenty and fifty hours if I met them all separately. The group meeting means that all questions can be covered in one short gathering. In theory, a good practice. But the questions asked in those conferences are often moronic.

'How do you feel after winning your first Wimbledon? (and the second, third and fourth?)'
'When do you think you had it won?'
'How did you play today?'
'How old are you?'

'What tension is your racket?' are some of the queries that draw short responses. Questions about my age and racket tension are two that are particularly annoying because both are on public record and indicate the reporter hasn't done his homework.

My tag as a sphinx, I guess, comes from my not giving away more than I'm asked by the press, and that's not much. If I could speak in my own language, it would be much easier. To explain yourself in a different language is difficult. So if someone asks me a question, I prefer to make a short answer.

Gene Scott: The press conference is like a schoolboy biology lab' in which a frog is dissected. The press picks apart Borg's anatomy like so many amateur probers, often with awkward motions and fumbling hands.

How can reporters have it both ways by climbing all over John McEnroe, Jimmy Connors, and Ilie Nastase for boorish behaviour and yet deriding Borg for being emotionless and plastic? The Swede does all anyone could possibly ask of him on court. He is courteous, calm, and serious about his work. He never questions calls or baits his opponent. Every official loves to work on his matches because he puts umpires and linesmen so utterly at ease.

Ironically, this sporting quality, instead of helping him, actually penalizes Borg by costing him as many as half a dozen points a match. It is human nature to give a break to the complainer to keep him quiet. Any umpire who has ever worked on a McEnroe or Nastase match desperately wants the event to proceed without incident. If McEnroe goes up in smoke on a close call at the baseline and Borg is silent, there is a tendency to give McEnroe the benefit of the doubt just to keep the peace.

The umpire therefore has the luxury of catering to the grumbler at the good guy's expense, which means that Borg loses on the tight decisions at both ends of the court. One example: in the first game of his final match with Connors at the 1976 Wimbledon, Jimmy served what everyone at court side – except the linesman – thought was a fault. Borg said nothing. Ace Connors. Next game, Borg served an ace past Connors that was close – could have been good or out. Linesman signalled good. Connors objected and the umpire called fault overruling the linesman. Borg lost both decisions where he was surely entitled to one of the points and possibly both.

The press's only contact with Borg is at press interviews and on court where he is perfectly behaved, yet he is abused for not having personality. That is absurd. Bjorn has a wry sense of humour, is mature, kind and warm. He is no Rhodes Scholar but neither are Arthur Ashe and Cliff Drysdale, the tour's resident smart men. If you want to talk seriously about Descartes or the world situation, don't pick a tennis professional. If you want to get your ears pinned back in tennis, Borg's your man, and the licking will be administered by the physical talents plus the intelligence of the world's most decent sportsman.

Tests of Borg's stature are everywhere. No one can ever remember hearing an ill word spoken of him by his peers. He brings out the best even among the circuit's dodgier characters. There are never any incidents in his matches, because players are too embarrassed to dishonour an athlete they know will give them every break.

Judith Elian, the revered tennis writer for L'Equipe, has known Borg since he came to Wimbledon as a fourteen-year-old junior and remembered, 'even as a kid he had a sense of maturity. This probably was why he never became spoiled later by his glory and riches. Money and fame are distorting forces and you have to have an unusual balance in your temperament not to go crazy.'

The question I am most often asked is how I am so unemotional on court and why I never seem to get angry over bad calls. Well, I can go crazy over bad calls but I keep it inside. How? When I was twelve years old, I was throwing my racket all over the place and cheating all the time. I was a real nut case. Hitting balls over the fence – everything. My parents were really ashamed and finally refused to come to a single match.

Suddenly I was suspended for six months by the Swedish Association. I lived in a very small town and the news of my suspension spread quickly. People whispered behind my back about my being the 'bad boy' of Swedish tennis. I took it very much to heart and it was a devastating experience that I remember as if it were yesterday.

Now if my opponent cheats, or if I get a terrible call, I don't say a thing. Inside I may say it all. But if I objected out loud, I know I would get so flustered and turn red that I'm determined never to do it. I guess the memories of my humiliation have stuck with me so that I'll never again do anything crazy or unsportsmanlike in front of a lot of people. I'd hope I wouldn't anywhere, crowd or not.

I think I get over my losses pretty quickly, which must be part of the same family of emotions, and I don't gloat over my victories. Once a match is over, it's over. I don't carry either the pain or the glory with me for very long. For instance, the day after I lost to Roscoe Tanner at the 1979 US Open, I had a two-hour breakfast meeting with my manager, Bob Kain, at the Drake Hotel. 'Not many athletes would have adjusted to such a heartsickening loss so quickly,' Kain said. 'In fact, not many would still be in town.'

There have been incredible changes in the game since I started on tour. The main one is the quality of player is so much better. Five years ago, I played all the tournaments for two reasons. I wanted to make money and I wanted to please all the tournament directors. Now I just play the big tournaments, because the draws at even the small tournaments are just as tough as the big tournaments. Remember those two Wimbledons when I almost lost to Victor Amaya and Mark Edmonson in an early round? The draws are now filled with players better than Amaya and Edmonson were then, and it's tough fighting through fields like that week after week. It's not so difficult for Amaya or Stan Smith or Brian Gottfried, because they don't win every week. I'm expected to. That's why I'm cutting down to fewer events next year to see if I perform even better by focusing on a few major tournaments.

For example, I have never prepared for the US Open the way I prepare for Wimbledon. If I lose Wimbledon this year, I'm going to try like hell for the Open, because the 'majors' are now my most important goals. By pacing myself in this way I think I can play at least five more years. One day I'm sure I'll be tired of travelling, sick of hotels and planes and I'll probably end up living in the United States – most likely in Florida.

Once or twice a year I lose to a player ranked a hundred notches below me. When it happens, some people accuse me of not trying. One example was when, as the top seed, I lost to Bruce Manson in the first round of the 1979 Palm Springs Grand Prix. Let me explain what happened. On the Sunday night beforehand I had won the Pepsi Grand Slam at Boca Raton, Florida, three thousand miles away from Palm Springs. I left for California the next day, flew for six hours when the plane was suddenly directed back to Houston because of bad weather. Mariana and I spent the night in Houston and on Tuesday morning started again for California. I arrived at Palm Springs in the afternoon and went on court forty-five minutes later – and lost. Manson did play well. I tried but I was so tired I really didn't care if I lost or not.

There is no other sport in the world where the season is twelve months long, demanding travel across the globe and back half a dozen times a year. Team sports in America have a limited season and all travel is within the States; and similarly in golf the entire PGA tour is played exclusively in the States. A few top players may try their luck in the British Open, but that's about it. Some might ask why, if I was so exhausted, I didn't withdraw. In tennis there is no provision for withdrawal, barring an injury, without facing a stiff fine. Besides, the pressure from promoters is intense to get you there in the first place. Every tournament director would rather have me play and lose in the first round than drop out. That way they can save face when confronted by spectators or press with the alternative of a Borg 'no show'.

Another embarrassment was when I lost to Raul Ramirez 6–0, 6–1, in the 1978 Teheran Grand Prix. Ramirez is a talented player, so I might be upset by him any time, but the love and one scores were an indication that I was wiped out physically from travelling and playing too much. I wanted to go home. It's not an excuse, but rather an explanation, when I say that my type of game from the backcourt requires incredible concentration and patience. It is difficult to operate at this level of intensity all year long without a letdown now and then.

Certainly it is more difficult to stay on top once you've got there. You must prove yourself over and over again. There is a hollow feeling when the challenge of reaching a goal is gone. The goal now is to stay there. It's like looking for excellence in isolation.

I know that most players play their best against me and, in a sense, this annoys me. My shots are straightforward and not deceptive – until a man rushes the net – so a pro can plan and play his game.

Human nature is not happy with staying the same. There must be changes. Since the competitive challenge starts to fade with repetition, there must be a personal challenge from within me to keep winning major titles. The chemistry of a painter is different from that of a tennis player. The artist is not judged as harshly as a tennis player. The artist does not win or lose every day in such black and white terms as we do. Picasso did not have a 5–3 won/lost record against Van Gogh. On the other hand, I do have to live with my 5–3 record against McEnroe and try to see to it that the balance doesn't change.

I have a close relationship with my parents – maybe too close. I've lived with them for five years, like Vitas Gerulaitis and his family. But now that Mariana and I are getting married, we'll make the Monaco apartment our home.

Gene Scott: Mariana Simionescu was born on 27 November 1956, is 5′ 5″, 127 pounds, has blonde hair, brown eyes. She is a moderate to heavy smoker. She was ranked two in Romania for four years. She won the French Juniors in 1974 against Sue Barker and reached the last sixteen at Wimbledon in 1977. 'The best match I ever played was against Virginia Wade at Wimbledon. I lost 9–7, 6–3 but was really upset because Bjorn didn't come down to watch me play. He stayed on top of the tea room to look at my match so he wouldn't get swamped by two thousand autograph hunters.'

How I met Mariana is one of those ironies that amuses me. Do you remember the 1973 Wimbledon where I made up the story for the press that the Swedish junior champion, Helena Anliot, was my girlfriend so that the schoolgirl mob scene might slow down? Well, it wasn't hard to fabricate Helena as my girlfriend because she was! We went out together off and on for five years, and during the 1975

Life on the road. Mariana does not like me with a beard, but I think it's too much trouble to shave regularly. That explains why half the time the public sees me with a beard and the other half without it (above)   (*Credit: Art Seitz*)

One of Mariana's and my favourite pictures (beard or not) (below)

A requirement for me, whether I'm travelling or not (opposite)

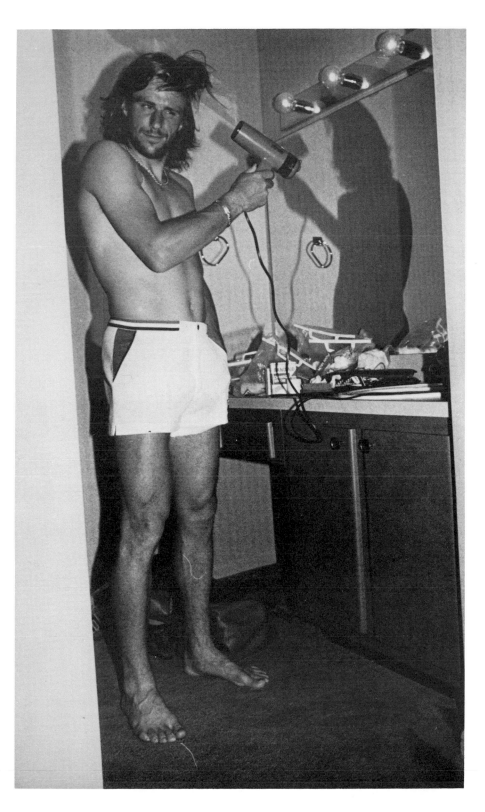

Bournemouth Tournament, Helena introduced me to her room-mate, Mariana. I wasn't impressed, yet I did remember her as shy and warm. The next year, after I had lost to Adriano Panatta in the quarter-finals of the French Open, Rune, my father, Lennart Bergelin, my coach, and I decided to go out and have a few beers to celebrate Lennart's birthday. We drove out of the hotel and after about five minutes decided we might be in such bad shape at the end of the night that we shouldn't drive home. We returned to the hotel and hopped in a taxi. But first I went into the lobby and on a whim called Mariana and asked if she'd like to join us on the bachelors' night out. Mariana hesitated, finally said yes, and we've been together ever since.

For sure, we've had our share of quarrels. Some of them are quite funny. Like the time at the 1978 Pepsi Grand Slam in Boca Raton, where Mariana, Lennart and I were sharing a suite. Mariana and I had a fight and she said she was going back to Romania. I said fine. She packed her bags and left. Two hours later, Lennart and I realised Mariana wasn't there to cook dinner. We panicked. Lennart volunteered to cook some hamburger meat, when, in the middle of a smoke-filled kitchen, the phone rang. Lennart answered and talked for a while and hung up. Ten minutes later Mariana appeared as if nothing had happened. We all laughed and Mariana went into the kitchen and cooked us a great dinner. She had taken a taxi to a hotel next to the airport and checked in before calling Lennart to see how the two men in her life were getting along.

In the beginning I believed you couldn't have a girlfriend and play good tennis. I've obviously changed my mind. I love Mariana very much, yet have no idea what it's like to have just one woman for my whole life. I think it must be very difficult. If you see each other every single day, I don't think it's good. Sometimes I go to play tournaments without Mariana – the breaks make me look forward to seeing her. Of course she is sometimes jealous. She knows there are women after me in each city for different reasons.

For the last three years we've travelled together all the time, which has meant Mariana couldn't play the circuit. For us it makes no difference if we are married or not. We live together like a married couple now.

Every time Mariana and I go to the States, Mariana orders an extra bed for herself so that I can get some sleep before the US Open. The record shows it obviously hasn't worked. She's become superstitious. At the 1980 Masters, she decided not to order the extra bed and instead

Mariana has been holding my good luck mascot since 1977 (left)   (*Credit: E.L. Scott*)

Mariana wears more than her heart on her sleeve (right)   (*Credit: E.L. Scott*)

stayed on the sofa at the Drake Hotel. The sofa was so uncomfortable that she didn't sleep for a week. But I won. I wonder what she'll do the next time I play in New York?

It helps that Mariana was a good player because she accepts the sacrifices. Another girl who doesn't know tennis might always want to go out dancing and to dinner. I can't do that and play my best tennis. Still I know it is a sacrifice for Mariana not to be able to have nights out on the town.

If I win, Mariana wins. Mariana appreciates what it takes to win and the preparation involved. Another woman might sympathize but Mariana's level of understanding is higher. She never ever interferes with my tennis. I know what to do or not to do with my game. It's good that she doesn't involve herself in how I'm playing.

Of course we joke around. Before one Wimbledon final, I asked, 'Scumpo, how should I play today?' 'Serve and come in', Mariana advised. Mariana's name for me is Scumpule and mine for her is Scumpo which means 'darling' in Romanian.

'I rarely talk tennis', Mariana explains. 'When we are alone it's the only time we are away from the courts. If we start talking about tennis it's too much. What sort of relaxation would that be?

'The reason Bjorn and I waited to get married was that we just didn't know each other in the beginning and were so young. A lot of youngsters know their girl friends or boy friends from high school or college. We decided to wait and find out about each other. We've been living together for four years and so getting married will be no different except that I'll be Mrs Borg and I'll call him my husband. And he'll introduce me as his wife. Some people don't seem to think it's a big deal to be married or not, but I think young people like the idea if they've found the right person. We certainly won't have children right away. It's too tough to travel with kids when Bjorn is on tour. Besides Bjorn's not ready to be a father yet.

'All the guys on the circuit are his friends but the only one he is close to is Vitas. When single men are on tour they tend to make a lot of friends while the pro women can be very bitchy outside their cliques. When I travel with Bjorn, he comes home right after he practises or plays, so he doesn't have a chance to build many close relationships.

'When he goes out on court, I don't know what he's thinking. No one knows. He may say that "I'm just going to play my game" but I can't tell what's really going on in his mind. Off court I know, for sure. And I think I know why he's so great. He's an unbelievable athlete and he's always in great condition. He sleeps so much and he doesn't smoke or drink – except some wine and beer during our rest weeks. Nothing tempts him when his tennis is involved.'

The other very close person in my life is my coach, Lennart Bergelin. My nickname for Lennart is Laban (Law-ber) which means monkey or clown in Swedish. At first he got very angry when we used it – now he knows it's just being affectionate. There is a lot of teasing in our friendship. For example, Lennart never lets the phone ring in my room when we travel. He screens all calls by telling the operator to switch them to his room. In this way I am not harassed by friends looking for free tickets, reporters looking for a story, or teenagers looking for some action. The phone rings so much in Lennart's life that he's become immune to the sound. Now when the phone rings on TV, Lennart gets up to answer it, but when it rings in the bedroom he's apt not to hear it. The guys in the Pro Shop a mile away could hear the phone it's so loud, but not Lennart.

Our most famous 'telephone' story happened in 1977 in Copenhagen, when Lennart and I sat in his hotel room waiting for room service. 'I have to call my wife', Lennart said. He dialled the number and nothing happened. He then called the operator and asked how to dial Sweden directly. She told him to push the white button and dial the number. Lennart saw a white button on the wall. He pushed it and the light above us went out and he dialled the number. Nothing happened. Then he pushed the white button again and the light came on and he dialled the number. Still nothing. He repeated the routine once more – the light going out – before I pointed out to him that there was a white button on the phone too, and why not try that?

Gene Scott: Lennart cares about Bjorn as if he were a bear cub. He thinks that the International Management Group pushes Bjorn too hard for exhibitions and he worries about an injury cutting short his career.

            'The exhibitions are killers', Lennart laments. 'At Frankfurt the match against Vitas ended at three in the morning with ten thousand people still in the stands.

            'It's easy to make the adjustment travelling from Europe to the States – two days and you're completely OK. The other way from Los Angeles to Monte Carlo can take a week of waking up at 1 a.m., then 4 a.m. and no more sleep. And rest

The score stands love – love (above)   (*Credit: Art Seitz*)

In Hawaii after the 1974 US Open. I wasn't always playing tennis (below)

Our wedding date will be recorded as 24 July 1980. Earlier, however, was the
bachelor party thrown by Vitas Gerulaitis at his condominium in Miami (opposite)
(*Credit E.L. Scott*)

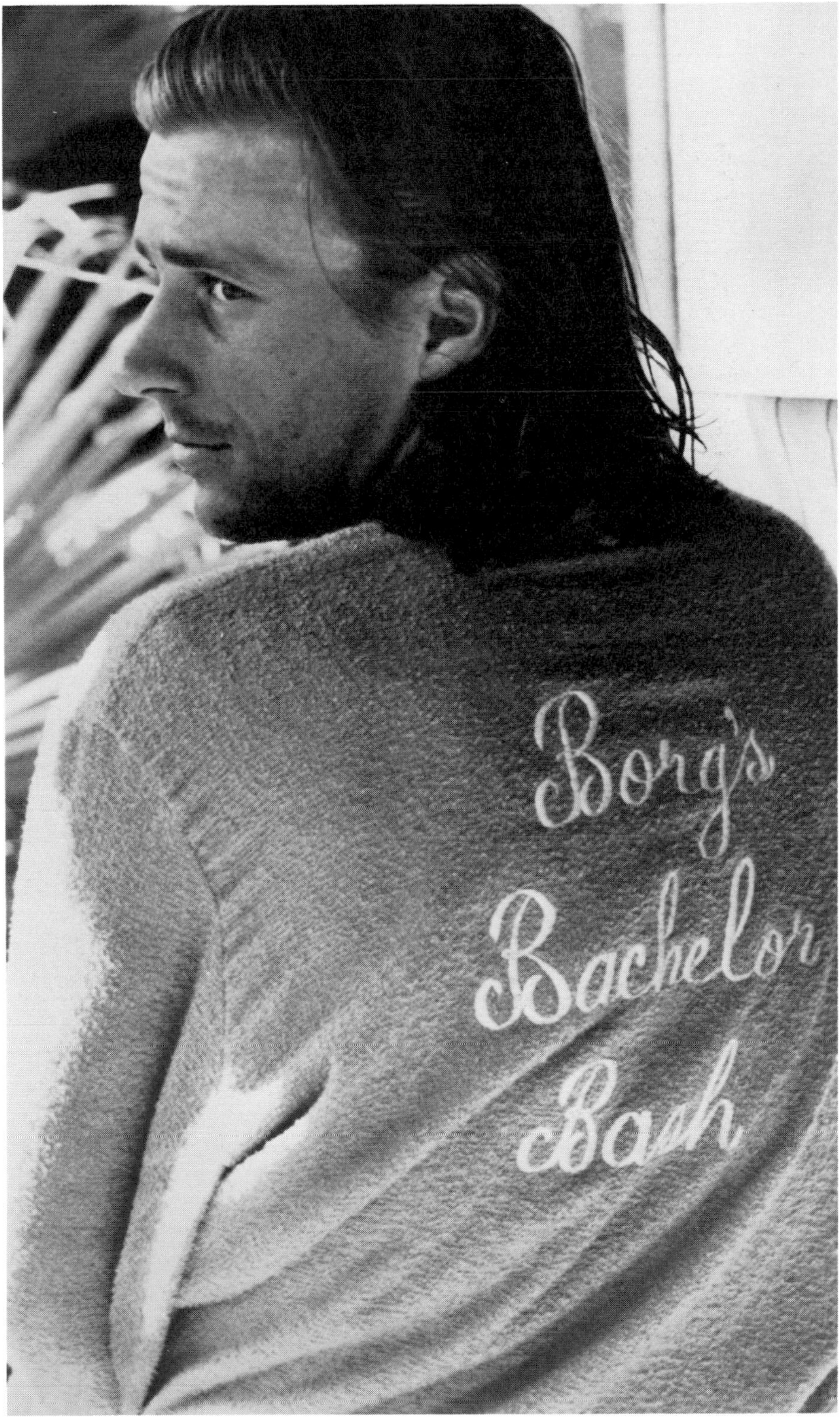
Borg's
Bachelor
Bash

periods to recover are non-existent.'

Borg disagrees. He has that flush of youth which makes him think he is immortal. Nothing can go wrong. If he has a week scheduled for exhibitions, he wants to play one every night despite the travel odyssey he must endure in the process. Here is an example of two weeks, from 25 February to 9 March 1980, in the exhibition life of Bjorn Borg.

Mon. 25 Feb.	Caracas	Mon. 3 Mar.	*Travel*
Tues. 26 Feb.	San Pablo	Tues. 4 Mar.	Copenhagen
Wed. 27 Feb.	Paraguay	Wed. 5 Mar.	Copenhagen
Thurs. 28 Feb.	*Travel*	Thurs. 6 Mar.	Munich
Fri. 29 Feb.	Chile	Fri. 7 Mar.	Munich
Sat. 1 Mar.	Chile	Sat. 8 Mar.	Stuttgart
Sun. 2 Mar.	Buenos Aires	Sun. 9 Mar.	Stuttgart

Followed by three weeks of rest.

It is estimated the two weeks will be worth a quarter of a million dollars tax free to Borg. The intricacies of arranging such a tour including iron guarantees that the money will be paid – in often less than stable countries – is part of International Management Group's expertise. Borg has a dozen Swiss corporations, off-shore funds, and tax free trusts to ensure that almost all taxes are avoided. That's true except in the US, which is the main reason Borg limits his playing schedule in America to tournaments only. There is no way for a foreigner to escape taxes on prize money earned in the United States.

My 'family' – mother, father and
Mariana (above) Lennart
Bergelin (below)
(*Credit: E.L. Scott*)

Statistics: Bjorn Rune Borg

Date of Birth:	6 June 1956
Place of Birth:	Sodertalje
Residence:	Monte Carlo, Monaco
Height:	5' 11"
Weight:	160 lbs
Eyes:	Blue
Hair:	Blond
Complexion:	Fair
Nicknames:	Scumpule ('darling' in Romanian), Burken ('can' in Swedish), Nalle ('teddy bear' in Swedish)
Beard:	From time to time
Marital Status:	Engaged to be married to Mariana Simionescu, Romanian professional tennis player, in Bucharest, 24 July 1980
Racket Brand:	Donnay, world-wide
Grips:	Forehand – western; Serve – continental; Volley – continental; backhand – two-handed eastern
Racket size:	$4\frac{5}{8}$ heavy, 10-inch fairway leather grip
Grip type:	Fairway – two leather grips per handle
Shoe Brand:	Diadora
Shoe Size:	$9\frac{1}{2}$
Shirt Brand:	Fila
Shirt Size:	Medium (40)
Short Brand:	Fila
Short Size:	32
Personal Habits:	Always wears on right hand gold bracelet with 'Bjorn' engraved in a small square, and a gold chain around neck (both birthday presents from Mariana), plus headband close to eyes. Sweatlets on both hands plus tape over knuckles and inside callous on left hand. Uses sawdust to dry hands, never gauze or glove. Wears thick wedding band on ring finger of left hand. Mariana wears duplicate as engagement ring, but a narrow band will be substituted on their wedding day

Career Earnings (1973–March 1980): $3,160,516. Does not include endorsements or exhibitions.

2. My life in tennis

I was born in Sodertalje (pronounced 'so-der-tal-yeh'), a small manufacturing town of 100,000 people thirty minutes south-west of Stockholm on 6 June 1956, which is Sweden's Flag Day. You might say I started celebrating early.

I am my parents' (Margarethe and Rune) only child and like many Swedish youngsters my first love was ice hockey. At nine, I was the starting centre for Sodertalje's junior team and had visions of playing for the national team when I grew up.

My father was one of the country's leading table-tennis players, and in the summer of 1965 captured the city championships, winning a tennis racket as first prize. He gave it to me. My first tennis racket at the age of nine. The next morning I walked four blocks to the Sodertalje Tennis Club and was turned down for the beginner's class because it was too crowded. During the next six weeks, I did what every aspiring tennis player does to learn the game. I attacked our garage wall with a vengeance, using it as a backboard. Every day I played imaginary matches between the USA and Sweden with the rules being that if I didn't miss the ball for ten hits, Sweden won the point. Then a vacancy opened up in the junior programme. For the rest of the summer I arrived at the tennis court at 7 o'clock in the morning and wouldn't leave until my parents collected me at dark.

The role of my parents was perfect. They were helpful but never interfered with my tennis. I was obviously crazy about tennis from the beginning and they gave assistance all the time but never told me what to do, when to practise, when to play tournaments. If they had become too involved, I would have quickly been sick of training, everything.

It's fine for parents to give guidance when you're younger, but once I was eighteen I knew for myself what I had to do to be good. It's like taking piano lessons when you're very young. If they had told me I had to practise four hours a day and pushed it down my throat, I would have quit tennis.

The next summer, when I was ten, I met Percy Rosberg, the best

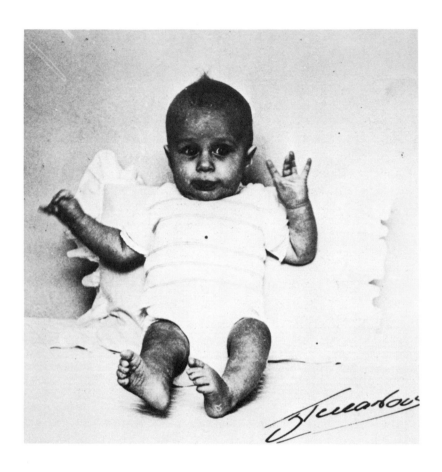

My earliest portrait

With my father and mother, Rune and Margarethe, in the grocery store which I owned in Sweden until the family moved to Monte Carlo

coach in Sweden, who came to Sodertalje to scout two thirteen-year-old juniors, Peter Abrink and Leif Johansson. I got a chance to hit with Percy for half an hour and he didn't seem too happy about my forehand, which I already hit with a western flick, the result of my father's ping-pong influence. But he saw that I could hit a lot of balls back and asked me to train with him at the Salk Club in Stockholm. Soon I started going to Salk seven days a week. Five of those were training with Percy and the other two were banging the ball about with anyone who'd hit with me. I travelled by train from Sodertalje to Stockholm for an hour and a half every day after school for five years. My parents would drive and pick me up at night, but I still wouldn't get home until ten o'clock.

When I started tennis, for two years I played all the shots with two hands – simply because my racket was too heavy. At the Sodertalje Club, every member said I ought to change my strokes. Finally I did change to hitting my forehand one-handed, but that wasn't enough. They wanted me to switch on the backhand too. 'You'll never amount to anything with that two-handed shot', they all said. 'If you want to be a big player you have to hit the backhand one-handed too.'

The members got angry with me because I obstinately refused to listen. In the end, I think that's the reason I've got so far. It was important that I was satisfied with my game. I was hitting the ball well and beating some pretty good players when I was very young, and even though I'd tell them that some day I'd change, inside I knew I never would. Eventually I did convert my forehand because it seemed so much easier to hit topspin with one hand than with two.

Between the ages of ten and thirteen I lifted weights twice a week for hockey, not for tennis. Since then I haven't lifted a weight. It probably does help some players with their arms and wrists but I don't need the extra muscle. The hockey helped me a lot with conditioning. It's good if you can play a lot of sports when you're young and then, when you get older, pick just one. Incidentally, it's also fun.

I won my first tournament the next year at eleven, when I beat Lars Goran Nyman in the Sormland County Championships. (Every tennis pro can remember his first tournament win.) The next summer I won my age division in the Swedish National School Championships. And the following summer at thirteen, I travelled to Malen, in the south of Sweden, for the National Junior Championships, and I won both the thirteen and fourteen age divisions. I was on my way.

When I was fourteen I was selected to represent Sweden in a junior

The influence of my early passion for ping-pong is still evident in my tennis strokes

I'm the one kneeling, second from left, but I gave up my first love, ice hockey, when I was fourteen

tournament in Berlin, which gave me my first experience of international travel. I was hooked. With some sadness, I dropped hockey to dedicate myself totally to tennis.

There was only one obstacle: school. The nickname given me by the girls in my class was Nalle or 'teddy bear', but my teachers thought I was behaving more like a grizzly. In the second term of Blombacka School's ninth grade, I fell way behind in my work as I was concentrating more and more on my tennis. One lady geography teacher in particular had no patience with me and told me in front of the class that I was 'lazy and stupid'. I baited her and later refused to answer any questions, saying that she was right – I knew nothing. This possibly was my earliest training for press conferences.

The headmaster said it was impossible for a fifteen-year-old to leave school, but finally, after pressure from my parents and Leif Dahlgren, a top coach for the Swedish Tennis Association, the school relented and let me leave in March 1972 just in time for me to take off for the Madrid Grand Prix. There I scored the biggest win of my life over Jan Erik Lundquist, a national tennis hero in the twilight of his career, in straight sets 6-3, 6-2. As a result I qualified for the Davis Cup Team in May against New Zealand.

My first assignment was against New Zealand's number one, Onny Parun, who preferred to serve and volley on grass than to rally from the backcourt on the clay courts of Bastaad. But he was physically strong and I was a definite underdog. The match started according to form and I dropped the first two sets, which took just over an hour, and was quickly down 3-1 in the third. At the 3-2 changeover Lennart Bergelin, our Swedish Davis Cup captain, took my racket and said, 'God that's heavy,' and gave me another one. I broke serve and won five straight games and the next two sets. I got unbelievably tired in the fifth set and was behind 3-0 before Lennart told me to play Parun's forehand more and to keep the points going. Parun was in good shape but he didn't like to rally for ever.

My tactics then were the same as now. Keep the ball in play and don't make any errors. Slowly Parun began to lose concentration and after two more hours his game had unravelled entirely. I came from behind to upset Parun 4-6, 3-6, 6-3, 6-4, 6-4, and became the youngest person ever to win a Davis Cup match. (Haroun Rahim was fourteen when he played for Pakistan in 1971, but he lost.) Two days later I won my second Cup match, defeating Jeff Simpson 9-7, 6-4, 5-7, 6-1.

I loved the fact that the scene of my first Davis Cup glory was in

Bastaad, a small seaside resort whose off-season population of 2,500 swells to 20,000 in the summer. Bastaad became the centre of Swedish tennis through the generosity of King Gustav V, who was an avid tournament player himself, and later through the patronage of his son, Gustav VI, who played singles at the Bastaad Tennis Club into his eighties.

My reputation for being cool under pressure started in the match with Parun. In the fifth set, I got a terrible call and didn't react. I told the press later that I wasn't bothered by referees or bad calls – that I just went after the next point. It was this response that caused the Swedish press to say for the first time that I had '*is i magen* (ice in my stomach)' but I wasn't always that way.

What was most important about my first Davis cup experience was that it brought me into close contact with team coach and captain Lennart Bergelin. During the try-outs I was losing a challenge match to Ove Bengtson and questioned three of Lennart's calls. I even called him a cheat, at which point Bergelin went berserk, pushing me over the courtside benches and hurling a racket at my head. I quit the match in tears and refused to practise for two days. The press criticised Lennart for 'bullying his players' and 'harsh discipline', but the complaints disappeared when he named me for the team.

The Davis Cup training period wasn't the only time my temper got out of hand that year. I guess the fifteenth and sixteenth years are rough periods for succumbing to tantrums for many players. A month later I went crazy in the Championship Cup against Leif Johansson, my rival neighbour from Sodertalje. In front of national television cameras I questioned a call by stomping over to Leif's side of the court and circling the mark where my ball had hit. I lost the decision and the match. The press wondered whether Borg's true character was coming out. But that was the last real display of poor sportsmanship of my career. I was embarrassed by my conduct almost immediately, but even more rueful that it had so upset my concentration that I lost the match.

If sixteen was an uneven age for my behaviour it was also an erratic age as far as my performance was concerned. I had some good results but nothing spectacular. I did beat Ove Bengtson in the finals of the Swedish Nationals to become our youngest champion, but most of my efforts consisted of getting close – like losing to Roy Emerson in the US Championships in four sets. The next season, 1973, was still unpredictable but now my youthful promise had taken a definite shape.

Congratulations from Gustav VI, the King of Sweden, at the Bastaad Tennis
Club in 1973

In the French Championships a few weeks before my seventeenth birthday, I upset the seventh seed, Cliff Richey, in the first round 6-3, 6-2. His game fitted mine perfectly. He couldn't outlast me from the baseline and he wasn't forceful enough on his approach or volleys to prevent me from getting a solid whack at my passing shots. Next, I edged Pierre Barthes, 6-3, 1-6, 8-6. The French hero was far flashier than I was, but when it came to the crunch he wasn't steady enough to play the percentages properly. Then I upset the US Davis Cup star, Dick Stockton, 6-7, 7-5, 6-2, 7-6. Americans never do well in Paris. The last one to win was Tony Trabert in 1955, over twenty years ago. The French clay is slower than the American Har-Tru or Fast-Dri, which means patience is at a premium. That's not the virtue of big servers and volleyers like Stockton.

The round of sixteen, against Italian idol Adriano Panatta, was another matter. Here was a man who understood perfectly the subtleties of European clay. Not only did he have excellent touch and feel from the backcourt but he was versatile enough to be a superb volleyer as well. Panatta won in four sets 7-6, 2-6, 7-5, 7-6, and I played as well as I knew how. Panatta is an extraordinarily gifted athlete, but although he is one of the few pros ever to win the Italian and the French Opens the same year (1976), he hasn't the discipline to take advantage of his talents consistently. On pure ability – particularly the effortless style of his groundstrokes – he is the one player who should be able to give Jimmy Conners, John McEnroe and myself nightmares, but he rarely does.

A few weeks later, I went to Wimbledon in the infamous year of the player boycott. Nikki Pilic, the Yugoslav star, was banned from Wimbledon by the ITF because he had refused to play Davis Cup for his country. The ATP (players' union) protested against the ban saying that players were free agents and should not be coerced into any competition. Battle lines were drawn between the ITF and all national associations on one side and the pros on the other. A court battle ensued which the ITF won, but the ATP still decided to pull its members out of Wimbledon. It was a tribute to the depth of men's tennis that the Championships went on as usual and broke attendance records despite the withdrawal of seventy-nine ATP players. Only two ATP members ignored the boycott, Roger Taylor and Ilie Nastase. Taylor felt a conflict of loyalty between his union and his birthright, Wimbledon, and chose his country, later suffering the wrath of his peers. Nastase, always controversial, told what the ATP considered more than a white lie, saying that the Romanian government had ordered him to play.

Only one Swedish player, Ove Bengtson, was a member of the ATP and he was the only one who withdrew. I played and was seeded fifth, opening my first men's match (I had won junior Wimbledon the year before) against the Indian, Prem Lall, on the famous Centre Court. I won 6-3, 6-4, 9-8 (Wimbledon had its own tie break at 8-all until 1979, when it joined the rest of the tennis world by starting the breaker at 6-all).

I remember thinking how lucky I was. Hundreds of players came to Wimbledon year after year and never got a chance to compete on the Centre Court. In my first match I played and won on the most famous surface in the world. In the next two rounds I defeated the German Karl Meiler and the Hungarian Szabolcs Baranyi, both in five sets, to face Roger Taylor in the quarter-finals.

The press went crazy over my success although it hadn't been that great considering the diluted field. The most famous headline during the fortnight appeared under Peter Wilson's byline in the *Daily Mirror* – A STAR IS BJORN. I lost to Taylor in five sets 6-1, 6-8, 4-6, 6-3, 7-5. I had been down 1-5 in the fifth and fought back to 5-5, 40-30 on my serve, when I was foot-faulted on a second serve, bringing the score to deuce. My concentration was shaken a little, and Taylor must have felt he'd been given a huge Christmas present. He won the next two points and served out the match, after sportingly overruling a service linesman who had called a ball in his favour on match point.

Later in the summer of 1973, I pulled off my best win over Ken Rosewall in the round of sixteen at the Canadian Open 2-6, 6-1, 7-5. Rosewall, despite being thirty-eight years old, was ranked three in the world at the time, and I had come back from 3-5 in the last set. I lost in the quarter-finals to Manuel Orantes 7-5, 7-6, but played well and heard Orantes say afterwards that it was one of his best matches of the year.

While I wasn't winning any tournaments, I was compiling a reasonable record of wins against higher ranked players and felt that it was only a matter of time before I could string together more than one good win a week. And my most unexpected victory of the season came ten days later at the US Open at Forest Hills – one of the last times it was played on grass. I upset Arthur Ashe, an expert on any slick surface, in the third round 6-7, 6-4, 6-4, 6-4. It was the first time I had beaten a superstar on turf. I wasn't supposed to win. My serve was weak and I had a non-existent volley. But I could hit groundstrokes all day and my passing shots were deadly. The pitch at Forest Hills was the worst of any major tournament, which actually helped my game. There is nothing so helpful to a slow spinning serve as a patch of bad grass. In addition, the court was soft, which meant that my shallow volleys stayed low, preventing Ashe from taking a big swipe on his passing shots. The experience was critical in building up my confidence that one day I could play well at the Mecca of grass tournaments, Wimbledon.

I always loved to play Ashe. Not that I always won. I didn't. The last match I lost at Wimbledon was to Ashe in 1975. He comes in on everything and anything on a fast or slow surface, so the points are over really quickly either way. He takes my second serve and chips it with his backhand to my backhand and lopes into net where I either pass him or he volleys a winner. I love to return his serve. It's hard and fairly flat, which gives me a perfect ball to hit – unless it's an ace. Ashe is clever when he plays – he uses his head. They say I don't talk a lot. What about him? I rarely get anything out of him.

For a long time I never concerned myself about the big money in tennis. The ITF prohibited any one under eighteen from accepting prize money, a rule which was abolished when I was seventeen. During the winter of 1974 I was tempted into signing an exclusive contract with World Championship Tennis (WCT) which organizes many of the major pro tournaments around the world. The Swedish Tennis Association was horrified that I would be lost forever from the Davis Cup, and so the President of the STA, Mats Hasselquist, devised a scheme where I would be hired by Scandinavian Airlines for five years and paid $100,000 a year plus free travel around the world as a public relations officer in return for playing the major Swedish tournaments plus the Davis Cup. I also could play any WCT events that did not conflict with my commitments to the Swedish Association. Simultaneously the maverick manager of Jimmy Connors, Bill Riordan, offered me a contract to play his USTA Circuit, but I turned him down feeling that even without Connors, WCT offered the best overall competition.

1974 was the first year I was a factor at every tournament. Two weeks after losing the WCT finals to Newcombe in four sets in early May, I became the youngest player ever to win the Italian Championships. I played like a streak, winning my last three matches over Orantes, Vilas, and Nastase. A week later, at eighteen, I became the youngest ever to win the French Open, beating Raul Ramirez, Harold Solomon, and then Orantes again in the final, after being down two sets to love.

I was wiped out physically and mentally by the time I reached Wimbledon and was destroyed by Ismail El Shafei, 6-2, 6-3, 6-1 in the third round. It was as if I wasn't there. I had one other poor result that year, losing to Vijay Amritraj in the second round of the US Open in five sets. But I beat Adriano Panatta at Bastaad, and Jan Kodes and Tom Okker in the US Pro in Boston. By the end of 1974 I was ranked three in the world and had earned $215,569 on court. Off court, giant offers for clothes, rackets, cars, beer, shoes and hotel endorsements tumbled in so fast that I needed an agent, so I signed with the American manager, Mark McCormack, whose clients at International Management Group included Arnold Palmer, John Newcombe, Rod Laver, Pele, Jackie Stewart, and Jean Claude Killy.

When I turned pro at the beginning of the year, I interviewed Bill Riordan, Donald Dell, and IMG for the best agent to represent me. Riordan had his own circuit at the time and was a maverick tennis promoter, but I always liked his sense of humour. Dell represented many of the top Americans but no prominent foreigners. Laver persuaded me to sign with IMG. For me they're the best. When I play exhibitions around the world it is important not to play in countries that have giant taxes.

Bob Kain of IMG looks after me in America – he's the best of all the agents – and Peter Worth takes care of me in Europe. Vitas Gerulaitis once almost lured me away from IMG to set up our own company. It was pretty close. Then I decided I had been with IMG for so long and they had been so good why should I get into the hassle of changing? IMG's full range of services includes five insurance policies covering injury, death and disability for the rest of my life. They have even bought a ten million dollar key man policy for themselves so that they won't lose future fees if I get hurt.

My proudest moments in the 1975 tournaments were victories at the French Open and the US pro – both for the second straight years – and the Davis Cup Challenge Round. But I vividly recall my defeat at the hands of Arthur Ashe in the quarter-finals at Wimbledon, 2-6, 6-4, 8-6, 6-1, the year he won the championship. Still it wasn't a bad year. I ended up ranked three in the world and $220,851 richer in prize money.

Overall that was a time of consolidation for me. I moved from

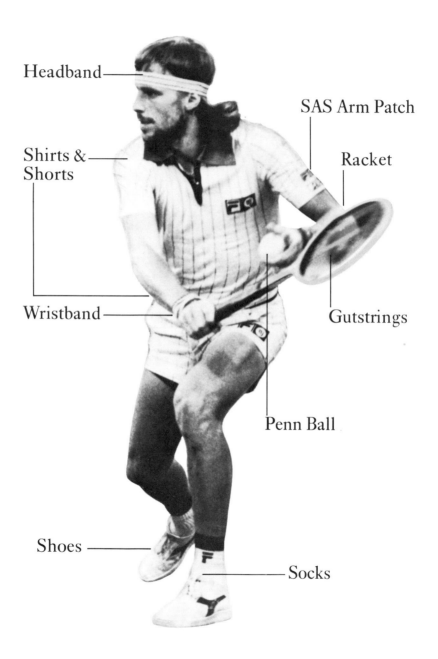

Headband

SAS Arm Patch

Racket

Shirts & Shorts

Gutstrings

Wristband

Penn Ball

Shoes

Socks

Stockholm to Monaco with my mother and father to avoid the 90% tax bite Sweden was taking from my prize money. Rune and Margarethe helped me open the Bjorn Borg Sports Boutique on the main street in

Bjorn Borg's Empire of Endorsements

Worldwide
Fila clothes (except Scandinavia)
Scandinavian Airline System
Diadora tennis shoes (except United
    States and Canada)
Tretorn clogs
Lois bluejeans
V.S. Gut
Saab cars
Power Swing teaching aid
Toy ball machine
Ektelon stringing machine
Bjorn Borg poster (two kinds)
Bjorn Borg calendar (two kinds)
Donnay rackets
Bjorn Borg jigsaw puzzle
Viking sewing machine
Suntan lotion (pending contract)

Canada
Collegiate headbands
Tretorn tennis shoes

Scandinavia
Bjorn Borg headbands
Jockey clothes
Bjorn Borg key ring
Bjorn Borg notebook, pencil and
    rubber

Europe
Penn tennis balls
Pelican tennis toy
Kellogg cereal
Tom's chocolate bar
Bjorn Borg doll
Cosmetic line (pending contract)

South America
Penn tennis balls

United States
Tretorn tennis shoes
Diadora running shoes
Caesars World properties
Bjorn Borg doll
Nutrament foods

Brazil
Bjorn Borg toy
Bjorn Borg soft drink

Japan
Sunkist soft drink
Department store boutique

The photograph of me on the facing page shows which bits of my equipment are endorsed annually by my major commercial connections.

Monte Carlo, where the weather was warm and the airport more convenient to allow me to jet to my tournaments around the world. I took absolute hell from people for leaving Sweden. I was called unpatriotic, selfish, and money-hungry by the Swedish press, which didn't ease my distrust of tennis writers. The only thing that turned their slander to praise was when Sweden won the Davis Cup. I won

Sweden captures the 1975 Davis Cup. Left to right, Ove Bengtson, Birger Anderson, the captain, Lennart Bergelin, and me

twelve singles matches over the teams from Poland, Germany, Russia, Spain, Chile and Czechoslovakia while not losing any, which is still a Davis Cup record.

I love playing for the Davis Cup. The last match I lost was in 1973, when I was sixteen, to Orantes, 6-1, 6-2, 6-1. I enjoy being a member of the Swedish team, despite the pressure of playing for my country. Our team would be better if someone else trained to play doubles. I'm not a great doubles player, but Bengtson and I are the best in Sweden.

One of my weirdest experiences in the Davis Cup was in 1975 when we faced Poland in Warsaw. Because of the strict WCT rules, I had to be in Dallas for the WCT finals for a mandatory press conference the following Monday morning. The only possible way for me to make connections, even with a private jet to London, was for my match with Wojtek Fibak to end at 3 p.m. on Sunday. If it wasn't over by then, everyone agreed I had to default. Sweden was leading in the tie 2-1 and needed my point to assure its win. The pressure was crazy. I won the first two sets 6-4, 6-1 when it started to rain. The Polish coach and captain told us to stop, but Fibak was very fair to me and played on. I won the final set 8-6 at two minutes to three. I didn't even change my tennis clothes. I put on my track suit and took a limousine to the Warsaw airport, where a waiting jet flew me to London. A TWA 707 was scheduled to leave at 5 p.m. We landed at Heathrow at 4.55 and taxied right up to the TWA jet. The TWA pilot knew what was up and stalled for five minutes. I ran my bags up the stairs, the stewardess closed the door behind me, and we left. Obviously the rule was absurd, but I didn't have the confidence then to tell WCT owner Lamar Hunt that the Davis Cup is more important than a press conference.

Birger Anderson was the hero of our team that year, winning one do-or-die match every tie. Against West Germany, the score was 2-all and he beat Karl Meiler in straight sets in Berlin. He won the decisive point against the Russians in Yurmala. Then we played Spain in Barcelona and he beat Jose Higueras in the fifth match in five sets.

In the challenge round against Czechoslovakia I couldn't sleep for three days beforehand. Bengtson and I played the best doubles match of our career and beat Kodes and Zednick 6-4, 6-4, 6-4, and I won my two singles. Sweden won the Davis Cup for the first and only time in its history.

Afterwards we went out to celebrate in Stockholm. Lennart had long woollen underwear decorated with tigers that he wore for good luck for every match, regardless of the fact that it was 100°F in Spain and Russia. He wouldn't take them off. At the end of our party, Lennart jumped up to dance on a table and took off his trousers to display his undefeated tiger underwear.

In 1976 for the first time I started winning tournaments almost at will. I lost some important ones, notably the US, French, and Swedish Opens, but I won more than my share, including the Canadian, WCT, German, US Pro and, of course, Wimbledon, without losing a set.

It was also the first year that I got power into my serve. I shifted my left foot position so that my toss wouldn't shoot all over the place. Now I had to hit the ball out in front. I gained rhythm, consistency, and power. I didn't watch anyone to get it right. I just practised serving one or two hours a day until I found out. I had never done that before. At the year's end, I had moved up to number two in the world and had won $424,420.

The next year my game was extraordinarily consistent. I had some major disappointments, again particularly in the US Open, but my percentage of wins was 92.2%. I won seventy-one matches and lost only six, the top record in the world. Wimbledon was certainly my most thrilling accomplishment, when I defended my title in a wild five-set final against Jimmy Connors, and for two weeks in August moved Connors out of the world's number one ranking. My official prize money count for the year was $337,020, which did not include $300,000 I made playing World Team Tennis for the Cleveland Nets for sixteen weeks. WTT had pursued me as early as 1974 to sign a contract, but Lennart thought the peculiar scoring system (one-set matches, 1,2,3,4 points), the endless travel, and the overall circus-like atmosphere would not be helpful at my stage of development. There was a general sentiment on the pro tour that WTT was positive security for older twilight players like Rod Laver, Ken Rosewall, and John Newcombe, but that the tournament grind was more competitive and better training. The one reason why I signed in 1977 was that Mariana was on the women's team and we could live together and play tennis without interruption. Very few tournaments have mixed fields now, and Mariana and I would have been separated most of that summer had WTT not offered us both contracts.

In 1978 I started out like a rainbow by winning the Italian and French Championships, and Wimbledon in a row – only the second player ever to do so. The US Open once again proved to be my undoing as I lost to Connors in the final. My ATP ranking slipped to three, but my prize money grew to $469,441. There are three or four semi-official sources for rankings in tennis, and it does seem odd that no single one is taken as official. The two largest tennis magazines – *World Tennis* and *Tennis* – separately compile records and come out with a year-end standing that is the judgement of their selected tennis writers. The ATP prints a ranking list every two weeks, which is the result of the statistics of the past twelve months as a whole. If you had a bad loss thirteen months previously, you might shoot up thirty places in the rankings when that loss dropped off the computer. Players are now very clever about beating the computer system and often can calculate how their ranking will improve drastically by sitting out a week. Even the US Tennis Association has a monthly computer ranking system, which is ignored by virtually everyone, although it is used to fix the rankings of the US players at the end of each year. It is ironical that for the past four years I have been ranked number one in the world by the year-end vote of the players, but only last year (1979) did the computer finally agree with that ranking.

1979 was the first time I started and finished the year ranked number one in the world on the ATP computer. My six best tournament weeks without question were the Pepsi Grand Slam, Wimbledon, the French, Canadian, and Tokyo Grand Prix, and the Masters. I won the Pepsi for the third time in a row, this time over Connors 6-2, 6-3. Then I barely captured the French Open and Wimbledon for the second straight year – no one has ever done this before, which proves how difficult it is to win on clay one week and grass the next. The finals of both could have gone the other way with newcomer Victor Pecci having already beaten Connors and Vilas in the quarter- and semi-finals of the French Open. I finally nailed Victor in four sets, but only after he had shown it is possible to serve and volley on clay if you have unusual talent.

I remember that they changed my locker-space at Paris for the first time. Lennart was so superstitious that he came to the attendant and shouted, 'What the hell is this? Why is it here and not here?' I stayed in the new locker and nothing terrible happened.

My seventy-three-year-old grandfather is also superstitious. During the French final, he and my father took their fishing boat out from Kattilo Island. They listened to my match with Pecci on the radio. If I won a point, my grandfather would spit nervously into the sea. Quite soon he thought I'd only win points if he spat. I won in four sets but he came back home with a terrible sore throat from spitting to windward.

I thought the Wimbledon final against Roscoe Tanner would be very tough. You never know how he is playing until you get there, he takes so many chances. I've never been so nervous in a match before. Everyone said I was going to win for the fourth time, which added extra pressure. When we started I was playing OK but not well and he was serving unbelievably. Tanner barely missed beating me, but I edged home 7-5 in the fifth set. Then I took an extended holiday in Monte Carlo and Sweden, mixing the beach with exhibitions all over Europe.

I returned in time to play the Canadian Open, which I won with surprising ease over John McEnroe in the finals. But it apparently didn't help my preparation for the US Open. Despite five-hour workouts with Vitas Gerulaitis for eight days before Flushing Meadows, Tanner got his revenge under the lights. I played well up to that point, and I'm not taking anything away from Tanner when I say his serve is improved by thirty per cent at night. You just can't pick it up early enough.

Assistant referee Bob Howe had assured Lennart two months earlier that I wouldn't have to play under lights. Then, on the first day of the Open, Lennart requested that, if I had to play at night, to schedule the games for the first few days and not for the Tanner match – we knew that would be the worst one, for sure. He was then told we wouldn't have to play under the lights at all. Apparently, they didn't think ahead and provide any good matches for the night time. When Jimmy Connors said at the last minute he wanted to play his quarter-final during the day, they put me on at night. It's history now that Roscoe put my lights out in four sets. He banged over a dozen aces and another dozen that I could only set up for his volley. My game on a fast surface is based on my return of serve. Take that away from me and I might lose to Tanner every time. I wasn't thinking about the Grand Slam. I wouldn't ever think about it until I had won three legs and had to change my plans to go to Australia at the end of the year, which is the time I normally rest.

Gene Scott: Borg is not given to making excuses for himself, but it is a matter of record that he has been unlucky at the US Open. In 1975, when he lost to Connors in the final, he was taking massive doses of antibiotics for an intestinal infection. In 1977, he lost to Stockton and had so bad a shoulder

Mariana and I celebrated my 1979 French Open triumph near the Eiffel Tower (opposite) (*Credit: Art Seitz*)

injury he could barely lift his arm to serve. In 1978, he lost to Connors after doctors had advised him not to play because of a severe thumb injury, for which he took two injections of morcaine, a powerful pain killer, an hour before the final. And in 1979, he lost to Tanner's 140 m.p.h. serve under lights, which may be worse conditions than any injury.

There was no need to think about Australia now. Just a few weeks of exhibitions and then the $300,000 Challenge Cup in Montreal followed by the Masters in January 1980, both of which I won. That totalled $290,000 for eleven days of tennis.

The Grand Prix Masters is promoted as the Super Bowl of Tennis – the last event of the year to decide the number one player (even though it comes in the middle of January of the following year). The argument that football's finale is scheduled the next year is not relevant. The American football season starts in September and is over after four months, apart from the Super Bowl. The tennis season lasts twelve months and then is stretched even further to accommodate a thirteenth for the Masters. It seems odd that we can't make a year of tennis last just a year.

The Davis Cup does the same thing. First round ties for 1980 were played before the 1979 challenge round was over. It seems ridiculous. Can't we organise a year's tournaments so they fit into twelve months?

After the 1980 Pepsi Grand Slam which I won last year beating Vilas and Gerulaitis ($150,000 for two matches), and the WCT Invitational in Maryland ($100,000 for six matches), I won't go back to America for six months until the US Open. It's not that I don't love the United States. Actually I like it so much that I may move to Florida before my serious playing days are over. The reason for not playing a full schedule there is that the tax burden is so heavy – fifty per cent Federal and in New York another twenty per cent – that it's simply not worthwhile to play tournaments or exhibitions beyond those I just can't or shouldn't pass up.

3. My rivals

Gene Scott: The casual spectator sees Borg as a blur of topspin forehands and backhands, often not understanding the components of the Swede's genius. When Borg trades strokes with Guillermo Vilas, for any particular instant, Vilas is his equal. What separates Borg from his rivals is best captured in their own words. Each has striven to find an offensive plan to penetrate Bjorn's immutable resolve, or a defensive one to frustrate his frozen concentration. Occasionally they are successful. More often they are not. But always they have a reaction to the experience of Borg stringing them out in endless imaginary lanes criss-crossing the entire court.

McEnroe on Borg

Left-handers will always give Bjorn some trouble. I think I have the perfect game to play him. Any two-handed backhand will be uncomfortable on my wide left serve. You have to mix up your pace. He likes the hard ball that Connors gives him.

He is always at the ball early. I'm not. He concentrates on the whole match, and, as at the Masters, if I let up for a few seconds and am late getting to the ball, he'll whip a few by me and the match is over [Borg beat McEnroe at the 1980 Masters 7-6 in the third set]. You must be in good shape to play him so you must prepare the entire match early and have the patience to mix it up with him.

'I've seen him a lot of times where it doesn't look like he's concentrating – at Wimbledon, for instance. You'd swear he wasn't trying when he was down two sets to Edmonson and Amaya. Maybe he was nervous and that's the way he combats it – with nonchalance when he's in danger.

I only met him three years ago when I got to the Wimbledon semis. But even in these three years he's developed a lot of personality. He's a lot more easy going. With the people he knows, he's comfortable, he's got a good sense of humour. With others he doesn't think conversation is necessary.

I think he's going to be on the tour longer than people think. Remember five years ago when the experts said that with his type of whippy game, his arm would be burned out in two years? Four Wimbledon victories later, he doesn't look slowed down to me. He's got a strong body and he can last indefinitely. It just depends on how much desire he's got. He's not going to play that much this year so he shouldn't get hurt. He's not 'over-tennissing' himself the way others are. He can afford to pick and choose his tournaments now – unless something unfortunate happens in the way of an injury. He's so successful at Wimbledon because the grass is not like a regular hard court. The surface looks after his volleys and makes them better than they are. He can hit a big first serve and stand on top of the net. He can drop volley or not even hit a solid volley and he'll win the point.

He stays back on his second serve and gets in a rally. He's the only guy I've seen who like to get in a rally from the backcourt on grass. It helps that he plays most of his matches on the Centre Court where the bounces are fairer and he can concentrate better. He's fast enough to be prepared early on grass too. He's faster afoot than I am, and, although Vitas is just as quick, he often seems out of position. Borg covers court better than Vitas. You don't catch Bjorn out of position too much.

At the Masters, I gave Bjorn an off pace short cross-court forehand three times. I figured ninety-nine out of a hundred times he'd miss it, but he made each one. I think I read him well, but you have to concentrate on every point or he'll pass you.

His serve? The first is damn good. He can hit that wide one in the deuce court and he can go flat. It's hard to pick it. I've played him when he's aced me once or twice a game. The second serve, he just gets in. But in the last two years he's developed more pace so it's harder to attack. When I first played him a while ago, the second ball would go to the same place at the same speed. Not now.

Sure we act differently on court. Once in New Orleans when I went berserk over a bad call he gently waved his palms up and down to calm me down. When we play, the match is always going to be interesting, because of our contrasting styles with me trying to rush the net and

John McEnroe   (*Credit: Kathy Finnerty*)

him staying in the backcourt. Sometimes when he and Connors play, it's dull because they both stay in the backcourt until someone misses.

The most satisfying place for me to beat Bjorn? The French Championships in Paris on clay over five sets.

Borg on McEnroe

His serve is the best. All left-handers give me trouble by serving wide to my two-handed backhand in the ad court which takes me way out of court. McEnroe builds his game on his serve. If he serves well, his confidence grows. If he serves badly his confidence drops quickly. He is incredibly fast. Great power volley plus touch with a flipping wrist. He can drop volley on both sides. It sounds strange, but he has more touch than Nastase. He is a master of the unexpected. I can never anticipate his shots. To beat him I have to keep him pinned to the baseline by maintaining perfect length on my groundstrokes. If I don't, he'll come in on anything. I'd rather play him on clay, but I beat John badly on cement in the Canadian Open two weeks before he won the 1979 US Open.

He says he gets bored playing from the backcourt against me. I don't think he gets bored. I don't think he has the confidence to rally from the baseline. If he stays back all the time, he's going to lose a lot of points. He has a great serve and volley, but he could improve his groundstrokes. We play a lot of exhibitions together and I've got to know him well. Despite what you read, he's a nice guy.

Connors on Borg

I played Bjorn seven times last year and didn't win once. Towards the end we had some good matches – one in Frankfurt, one in Montreal, and finally the Masters. My game was picking up and responded to my feeling better mentally and physically. When Patti was pregnant I was worried, and when the baby was born I wanted to spend a lot of time with him. My tennis suffered.

The adjustment was a big change for me. It took me time to separate my family and my tennis and to enjoy both.

To beat Bjorn I have to do what I do best. Attack. But I have to be more patient and can't miss after three or four balls – like at the Garden [Masters 1980] we were hitting fifteen or twenty balls a rally, which is what the people wanted to see. The tennis was unbelievable, and I don't think there was a loser that night. He won the match but the experience is going to help me against Borg six or seven months from now. It made me feel that I can play against him again.

I'm going to come in because he hits so many short balls. If I hit my groundstrokes deep and sharp, like I have been lately, he'll come up with a short ball more often than I do. We both hit the ball hard and it's going to come down to who misses an easy one here or there.

But I have to believe in myself that I can hit fifteen balls in a row so that I can wait for the short one. I have to be in good shape to run down balls and to move the ball around. I've been working on myself physically the last few months – three hours a day in Florida against Eddie Dibbs, Harold Solomon, and Fred Stolle who pound me into the ground, though once we get to the indoor circuit with the restrictions on court time we're lucky to practise thirty minutes a day.

I have no idea how Bjorn wins Wimbledon on grass. He's not so comfortable on hard courts or indoors – the natural place for volleyers
and then he wins Wimbledon four times on grass, which is even more natural a place for volleyers. I don't know whether it's a mystery to him too. Probably he's helped to some extent by the grass taking care of bad volleys – the short ones and the mis-hits are more effective than the good volley that gives your opponent another shot at the ball.

For pride reasons – he's beaten me in two finals – I'd rather play Borg at Wimbledon than McEnroe and the rest. McEnroe has a totally opposite game. He serves and volleys which gives me a target. McEnroe can stay back and hit groundstrokes but they're not as penetrating. Borg is predictable. He's not coming in much. Borg and I

Jimmy Connors   (*Credit: Jack Mecca*)

are the same in one respect; that we hit big enough approach shots that we don't have to hit a great volley. McEnroe will serve and volley constantly which puts me in more of a rhythm, though he's difficult because his shots stay so low. Borg is tough because he hits so many balls back. He must have so much confidence winning Wimbledon four times. But believe me, they're both tough.

Borg on Connors

We're not really friends. Not like Vitas. Connors is one of the game's quick men and he works hard for every point making him tough to beat. At first he intimidated me with his power and he had a strong winning record over me, but I think I played him wrong by trying the strategy of other pros – to hit slices, soft and short, to break up his rhythm. That was not my game. When I developed more confidence I felt I could hit the ball just as hard as Jimmy and yet I was steadier. That was my game. And it worked. I played him seven times in 1979 and didn't lose once.

Cliff Richey

Richey on Borg

Gene Scott: Cliff Richey was the top ranked American in 1970. He won the overall Grand Prix in 1970 and that same year was ranked number seven in the world. His sister Nancy was ranked number one in the USA in 1968 and 1969.

In 1973 I was playing the French Open and was seeded pretty high. Nancy was also expecting to do pretty well in Paris and asked me who I played in the first round. 'Some guy named Borg,' I answered. 'Never heard of him.' 'He's only sixteen.' I lost 3 and 2.

I had also asked Nancy who she was to play in the first round. 'Someone unpronounceable called Navratilova,' Nancy replied. 'Never heard of her.' Nancy lost 3 and 3.

It was my first and only meeting against Borg. He had huge groundstrokes. Compared to the other Europeans with good groundies – Pierre Darmon, Nicola Pietrangeli, and Manuel Santana – Borg had no variety, no drop shots. Just boom-boom. Even without variety he was good enough at seventeen to crunch most of the players.

I don't know about comparisons. You know, who's better, Rod Laver, or Bill Tilden, or Borg? Laver and Pancho Gonzalez at their peaks were too good to be rolled over by Borg. Pancho or Rod against Bjorn – all at their peaks? A helluva match no matter which.

Nastase on Borg

Borg plays like a pawnbroker. He doesn't give any points away. Never. Maybe he's the same way about his money. He's an unbelievable athlete. You remember when he competed in the Superstars television even in Vichy, Spain, he won six out of eight events including table-tennis, soccer, canoeing, and the 600-metre steeplechase run, in which he beat the 110-metre steeplechase Olympic gold medallist? His legs are very strong. He's like Ashe emotionally, quiet, shy. If you left him alone in the locker-room, he might not talk to anyone for an hour. But if you kid him, he's good and jokes back.

He can win when he's not playing so well – you know, hitting the ball off the wood, missing. Yet he keeps coming after you – so confident. Connors, on the other hand, can't win against the top guys when he's not playing well.

They should send Borg away to another planet. We play tennis. He plays something else.

Borg on Nastase

When I was eighteen or nineteen it was tough to play Nastase. I had no experience and got nervous waiting for him to talk nonsense to the crowd, umpires, and even me. Now I have played him so many times, I know what to expect and he doesn't bother me. Sure, we are good friends. But when I go on court, I don't care if it's my parents. I'm going to beat them. I've no hard feelings against Nastase when he behaves like a maniac. When we walk off court everything is fine and we're friends again.

In the beginning he was difficult to play because I never knew what he was going to do. Maybe he didn't either. Every stroke was possible. His shots went anywhere with all kinds of spin. Finally my serve got better so he couldn't attack and come in with that slice backhand approach which I hated. Also he used to let me come to net with short balls or drop shots because he knew I didn't volley with confidence. I practised the volley, serve, and pass off a slice backhand so much that Nastase couldn't hurt me any more. McEnroe is more of a total player in that he can serve me out of my socks in the backhand corner and can attack with variety, but no one had the versatility of counter-attack of Nastase. He could hit winners from the craziest defensive positions.

Ilie Nastase   (*Credit: Kathy Finnerty*)

Gerulaitis on Borg

He happens to have a pretty good game against me. To hurt the guy you have to serve really well, put away a lot of volleys, and play aggressively. Several times we've played it's been a close match, but he wins the big points – he does that against everybody! At Wimbledon in the famous match [1977 semi-final], I had a break in the fifth set and had a chance for another and also had a chance to hold my serve to keep the break alive, but he played good percentage shots each time. Played steady and made me make the error. He usually gets a high percentage of first serves in. The second one you can still attack but if you don't make a fairly good approach, you're dead, he has such incredible passing shots. I don't read him as well as some of the other guys do. McEnroe reads Borg like the front page.

I think Bjorn does have emotions but he has a special talent for masking them. He doesn't let his opponent know what he's feeling. I've never seen him change his expression in all the matches I've watched him play.

I've been there on an outside court when he lets off steam; but his emotions run at a low level and usually the most excitement you get is a faint smile, but that's his way and I appreciate it, even though I might go into hysterical laughter over the same thing.

He does have a great mental attitude but his strokes are sound too, despite people saying they're strange or unorthodox. When he's playing badly he'll just hit the ball a little higher and shorter, but it's always over the net. He always makes you play the ball. I've never had a negative attitude even while losing to him sixteen times in a row. I always go out thinking I can get him this time, because I've played so many close matches with the guy. I don't think for me it's so much of a mental thing. It's just that he knows my game so well – better than I know his game.

I think he's got a good chance for a fifth Wimbledon title. The pressure is off after the fourth in a row. Everyone is puzzled by how a clay-courter like Bjorn plays so well at Wimbledon. It's simple. First, he returns solidly, plus the grass makes his volley better than it really is. Balls that he hits short or mis-hits – flub volleys – are great volleys on grass. He also plays the bounces beautifully on grass. Everyone else is worried about bad hops, but they don't affect Bjorn. You need a lot of patience on grass because sometimes you get so frustrated with the way the court is playing, yet nothing fazes him.

Also he prepares his strokes so early – quicker than Connors – which gives him another edge on grass. He stays back a little extra on grass and yet is fast enough to cover all the balls that come short. He is a great retriever. He constantly keeps the pressure on because he returns everything. Most of us wait for cheap points on grass. Not Bjorn.

Borg on Gerulaitis

Compared to a few years ago, Vitas has improved so much on the baseline. I had a big advantage because he had no confidence in his groundstrokes. Previously, he had to come in all the time, either immediately behind his serve or waiting just a stroke or two. He's getting tougher and tougher – he's so much more patient in the backcourt. I can feel when we play matches now that he's a better player – even when I keep winning I sense this. Everyone says that his big improvement is in his serve. Certainly his serve is better, but the reason he's finally beaten McEnroe and Connors is because his forehand and backhand are steadier.

The fact that we practise together all the time has helped him in two ways – one that we hit hundreds of balls from the backcourt, and the other that he has learnt my game so well that it doesn't over-awe him. I won't keep beating him. Yes I've won sixteen times in a row, but that's the luck of our styles. His fits mine perfectly. I love players to rush the net on everything because it plays directly into my strength, my passing shots. Vitas is a steady and quick volleyer, not a 'put-away' volleyer, so I always get a second chance to hit a passing shot. If we hadn't practised all those times, the scores might have been worse.

If Vitas is playing badly, his forehand goes first. Then he backs up on this ball and hits it off balance. I think the reason I have beaten him is that he gets nervous against me. When we practise, he's not nervous at all and he serves better – everything is better. We're about even in practice – sometimes he beats the hell out of me.

Vitas is much more serious about the game now. I know he stays out late going to Studio 54 and the Mudd Club, but he doesn't drink or smoke at all so the next day he doesn't feel terrible, and can still go out and practise for three hours after sleeping ten hours until three in the afternoon. Also, he doesn't fool around during an important tournament. He's my best friend on the tour, except for Mariana and Lennart, and the one with whom I spend most of my time.

Vitas Gerulaitis (above)

Even in the Bahamas, teenagers flock to Gerulaitis and me. Same thing at Wimbledon (below) (*Credit: E.L. Scott*)

Vitas is my closest friend on the tour (opposite) (*Credit: E.L. Scott*)

Tanner on Borg

I'm not in awe of Bjorn. I respect him. I've beaten him and know I'll do it again. I have a plan whenever I play him and when it works, I win. I must serve and volley well. I must take his second serve, rap it, come to net and hit a good first volley. If I float my approach or volley, I lose. He's accurate, fast, and has quick hands at the baseline – not at the net. That's why you never see him at net.

He is the ultimate percentage player so it doesn't do me any good to stay in the backcourt and rally with him. He's the world's best at that game. I have to take chances. I don't mind if I miss, but I must take risks if I'm going to break down his percentages. I have a chance by taking a chance. Borg is the best not because of his picture strokes but because of his head. Connors has the purest shots.

I don't understand knock journalism. After Borg won four Wimbledons no writer was satisfied. After he lost to me in the US Open quarter-finals the press asked crazy questions of Bjorn, asking him if he was going down hill, tarnishing his incredible Wimbledon record. I don't know how he took it.

Borg on Tanner

I don't know him well. Maybe I should. He destroyed me at the 1979 Open and almost knocked me off in the finals of the 1979 Wimbledon. How I play against Roscoe really depends on how he is playing. He can beat anyone when his serve is humming. But he can lose to anyone too. He's just not consistent, which is worrying for me because I don't know what to expect. He takes incredible chances on his serve and groundstrokes and if he's on, I lose and if he's missing I'll win. Simple as that.

Roscoe Tanner

Vilas on Borg

Borg can run longer and faster than me. A few years ago when I was beating him, I was in better condition. But then he was still growing up physically, and not at his peak.

He doesn't play many tournaments these days and seems very fresh. He sleeps ten hours a day. When I lost to him so easily in the 1978 French Open I had had a tough path to the finals, and he had got there easily. I was sluggish and was always late to the ball.

It's better for me to play him on clay. His speed doesn't mean as much there because everyone has more time to run on slow courts. When I play Borg indoors I'm always off balance. I can't attack him easily and he can run forever. The only way I know to beat him is to wait for the short ball and come to net.

He's very good at adjusting to strange conditions. He'll just put the ball in the middle of the court with plenty of spin until he gets used to the surface, wind, etc. John Newcombe once said that Borg's arm would wear out in five years because he swings at the ball so hard. Nonsense. Borg's body is his best stroke.

Borg on Vilas

Guillermo is not as quick as McEnroe, Gerulaitis, Connors or myself. But we play the same type of game, except that I may do many things just a little bit better. Four or five years ago we used to practise together all the time. He was my best friend on the tour. Then Tiriac became Vilas's manager and our relationship changed. He hasn't seemed as open as before. Tiri even tried to change Vilas's game by making him serve and volley more. He doesn't seem to have the same confidence as when he was staying in the backcourt. His great winning streak in 1977 of ten tournaments in a row, including the US Open, was all on clay. His ranking has dropped to six in the world. Maybe he should return to playing like he used to. But I think Vilas needs someone like Tiri to lean on. It helps him mentally. When I play Vilas it's strange, because I feel that I'm stronger – which sounds crazy because Guillermo is such a bull. Yet I sense if we rally back and forth seventy-five times, I'm going to outlast him. Of course I lose a lot of points, but I have the confidence to stay with him forever. How can he hurt me? He can't serve and volley, and I can out-rally him.

Guillermo Vilas

Tiriac on Borg

Basically Borg is a more solid player than Vilas. You can beat Bjorn in only two ways, by attacking, or by outrunning him from the baseline. Vilas doesn't attack that well yet, and Borg is slightly better from the backcourt, so how can Vilas win? What makes the situation worse is Borg is so strong mentally. Normally, given Borg's slight stroking superiority, Vilas would win one out of three times, but because of his head, he loses eight out of eight times.

It sounds like a contradiction, but what makes Borg so tough is his lack of diversity. He knows two things – backhands and forehands. He can't get confused wondering when he should serve or volley or attack. Also he moves better than Rosewall. He gets to the ball way in advance, meaning he's both quick on his feet, and anticipates well.

The final ingredient that puts Borg in the untouchable class is his percentage tennis. Vilas plays the percentages from the backcourt but he's not as patient as Bjorn. Vilas is not just playing against Borg now, you know. We're all playing against his legend.

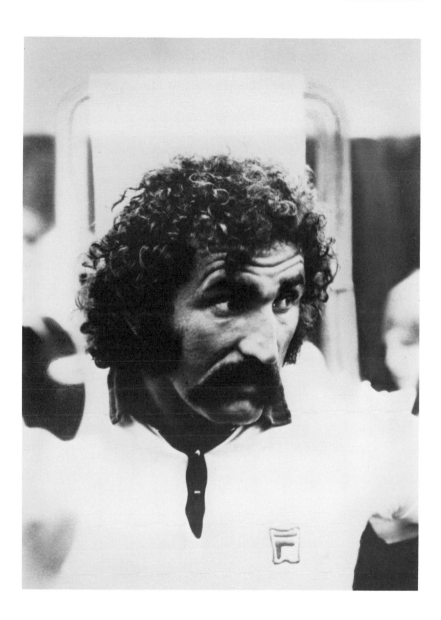

Ion Tiriac

Solomon on Borg

Borg is the best athlete in tennis. His combination of speed, stamina, concentration, and maturity on court is simply superior. I've played him fourteen times and never beaten him. In fact, I have only won five sets.

Maybe there's something wrong with him. The last time I played him for over three hours and changed my shirt four times, and I looked at him and his shirt wasn't even wet, and I've never seen him take a deep breath on court. I've tried everything. But each tactic I use he uses a better one, and he's faster and has more endurance. One basic reason why he can last longer is that he doesn't jump off the ground on making contact with the ball. His topspin bounces high making me leap up in the air to return. I'm always reaching and am off balance eighty per cent of the time. If I let the ball take its full spin it's over my head, if I take it on the rise I make mistakes. I can stay out all day with Bjorn and it doesn't alter the outcome.

The lefties and big servers give him problems, Victor Amaya, Mark Edmonson, Hank Pfister, Tom Gullikson, Tanner and McEnroe; but they have to strike when they get a chance because he'll close the door pretty quick.

Borg is a true champion. He's our best representative. The best thing that's happened to him is McEnroe. The challenge will keep him going for big titles for another five years.

I remember playing him in Tokyo in 1975. I won the first set 6-0 – just killing him. Tiriac came to the court and told Borg not to go for winners all the time. Borg won the next two sets 6-0, 6-1. He has animal instincts. His mind is clear enough for him to put it out of the way when he plays. He just lets it happen. Borg is an enlightened tennis player.

Harold Solomon

Martin on Borg

Gene Scott: Billy Martin of Palos Verdes, California, is only six
months older than Bjorn, and when they were
juniors they were heralded as the future of tennis.
Both won Junior Wimbledon (Martin won it
twice), and have beautiful groundstrokes. The
similarities continue down to their two-handed
backhands and the fact that Billy has married a
Swedish girl six months before Bjorn will marry
Mariana. As a UCLA freshman, Martin won the
National Intercollegiates in 1975 and experts
predicted a dramatic rivalry between Billy and
Bjorn and their sharing the international spotlight
for a dozen years. It never happened. Martin ranks
sixty in the world, Bjorn number one.

I remember playing Bjorn for the first time, in 1972 when I lost to him in
the quarter-finals of the Orange Bowl, 7-6, 5-7, 6-4. At 4-all, 30-all in
the final set, I came up to the net and my feet wouldn't move. He passed
me easily. I didn't win any more points. I was physically dead and he
wasn't even tired.

The next time I played him was in 1977 in Cologne and he thrashed
me 6-0, 6-1, but I had game point in nine games. I played for him to
miss at game point which is a big mistake against the best percentage
player in tennis. His confidence, his will, and his mental toughness are
the most awesome in the game.

Billy Martin

4. Coaching

'I think Bergelin helps Borg from a confidence point of view and he takes away Bjorn's worries, but I don't know how much he helps with strategy – not that he doesn't know about strategy, but that's not his role.'
Vitas Gerulaitis

Gene Scott: There have been nearly as many lines written about famous tennis coaches as about their pupils, and not much has been complimentary. The most common words used to describe Ion Tiriac's relationship with Guillermo Vilas are 'crutch' and a 'Svengali'. Part of this is the press's natural inclination to be sensational and negative – otherwise why wouldn't the first description of any coach be more positive, 'aid' or 'loyal friend'?

The bad name given coaches is directly attributable to the media reaction to the personality of one man, Ion Tiriac. Before Tiriac, coaches were behind the scenes and faceless. But because Tiriac's behaviour looks so sinister, first the players then officials ganged up on Tiriac. Did you know, for instance, that before the Tiriac/Vilas partnership, coaching on court during a match was legal?

In 1978, the International Tennis Federation adopted a no on-court-coaching-rule but properly it should have been labelled the 'no Tiriac rule'. Without a chain-smoking, snake-haired Tiriac staring at Vilas with a blank expression, but with hand gestures weaving wickedly at crucial moments during Guillermo's matches, there would have been no change in the rules.

The new rule is foolish. Partly because it's

> unenforceable. Who's to say that Tiriac's sneeze
> doesn't mean 'come to the net more', or that
> Dennis Ralston's tug on his right ear doesn't
> mean 'play your man's forehand'?

'Of course the rules were put in against us', Tiriac smiles. 'For that period in 1977 when we won eleven straight tournaments and fifty-eight straight matches, we were a helluva winning combination.

'Some parts of the game are more amateur than they ever were. Coaches could make the game go a lot smoother. The ninety- and thirty-second rules could be enforced better with coaches on court. If the coach interfered with play, the umpire could throw the coach out. At the moment referees are afraid of disciplining a player because the star gate attraction might be dumped from the tournament. Coaching has improved every other game. Why should tennis be any different?'

Roscoe Tanner agrees. 'The coaching rule is crazy. This is pro tennis. Why shouldn't coaching be allowed as it is in every other professional sport? The classic, absurd argument used to pass the rule was that since not everyone can afford a coach, they shouldn't be allowed. Based on that rationale, because a guy ranked 250 in the world can't afford to stay in a first-class hotel, I shouldn't be allowed to stay at the Hilton either.'

Gene Scott: It is ironic that of the top ten players in the world, only Borg (and his coach Bergelin) feel that on court coaching should not be allowed. Ilie Nastase was himself once coached by Tiriac, now he is just amused by how the whole issue has got out of hand.

'Last week at the 1980 Volvo Games in Palm Springs, I saw Tiriac coaching Vilas on every point against Billy Scanlon. Vilas would try to hit a passing shot and Tiriac – talking in Italian – would say "no, lob". No one seems to care about Tiriac's illegal coaching now, because Vilas isn't winning so much. I think it is a good idea to have a coach, in the sense that you have someone to look to during a match for moral support. He's a friend. Someone who always wants you to win.

'Tiriac has tried to change Vilas as a player from a steady baseliner to someone more aggressive. Now you see Vilas underspin his backhand and charge the net. Tiriac has taught Vilas about ten different service motions, trying to make his left-hander more effective. It's confused Vilas. It's silly. Vilas has played one type of game for fifteen years, and in six months, Tiriac thinks you can switch everything around.'

Gene Scott: Coaching is a critical and colourful part of
virtually every other game. Can you imagine
American football, basketball, boxing, soccer, or
baseball without the wild ravings of the
coaches?

Tennis coaches are divided into three
categories. Those like Nick Bolletieri and Dr Alex
Mayer who teach mechanics (grips, technique,
etc.); those who teach the mental side of tennis
(strategy, training, inspiration), such as Pancho
Segura, Harry Hopman, Pancho Gonzalez and
Fred Stolle; and, lately, another category has
emerged where the coach performs part, if not all,
of the manager's role. Tiriac is one example,
Borg's coach Lennart Bergelin is another.

Lennart Bergelin, 55, is thirty-one years older
than Borg. He is married with three sons –
Stephen, 31, an engineer; Erik, 28, who may
become a lawyer; and Nick, 14, still at school and
not a tennis player of any distinction. Lennart was
Swedish National Champion twice, and star of his
country's Davis Cup team for eight years. He won
the German Championships on clay in 1951. He
was coach and captain of the Swedish Davis Cup
team from 1970–75 but turned the job down in
1976 because the government took seventy per
cent of his coaching salary in taxes, and he
became Bjorn's full-time coach instead.

'I really started to coach Bjorn in 1972 when he first made the Davis Cup
team. I never believed a player could stay at home and become a champion.
You have to leave home and play tournaments so you can grow up to be a
match player, not a practice player. You can see pretty quickly who is a
tournament player and who is not. After a year Bjorn was getting seventy-five
per cent of my coaching even though I was coach of the entire team. I never
knew how good he was going to be, but the possibility for him to be the best
ever was there early on. We were together all the time anyway so there wasn't
much of a transition when I became his full-time coach in 1976.'

Gene Scott: Lennart, although a simple and quiet person, is
extremely outspoken on two particular issues. One

With Lennart Bergelin after I won the $100,000 first prize in the February 1980 WCT Invitational in Maryland (above)   (*Credit: E.L. Scott*)

Bergelin pinned Sweden's 'Athlete of the Year' award on me for winning the French and Italian Opens in 1974. Lennart himself is the only other tennis player ever to receive the award (below)

is the matter of exhibitions, which he feels are
wearing Bjorn down, and the other is that of the
US Open being played in part under lights.

'The US Open is part of the Grand Slam, supposedly the most important
tournaments in tennis', Lennart says. 'All the tournaments should be played
under identical conditions, except for the court surfaces. The French,
Australian and Wimbledon Championships don't have "two gates", one in
the daytime and one at night. These events should all be outdoor daytime
tennis. The nightime schedule totally fouls up the athlete. There is no other
sport where the athlete can finish at midnight and have to play the next
afternoon at 2 p.m. I understand the theory behind two gates, it's a way of
selling more tickets. I just don't think that's as important as fairness, and the
players' health.'

Gene Scott: Bergelin has strong views about the harm of
exhibitions on Borg's body. He had just watched
Bjorn lose the first set to John McEnroe in the
semi-finals of the 1980 Masters, and he muttered,
looking straight ahead, arms still folded tightly.

'Damn exhibitions, you can see it in his legs – tired. Four times a year, he takes
off on an exhibition "binge" where he'll play four matches in five nights all in
different cities. Each night he finishes at midnight and by the time he's had a
meal and gone to sleep, it's 2.30 a.m. The next day he has to get up at 8 a.m. to go
on to the next city. It's too much – the body doesn't recover from that sort of
strain easily. Bjorn's a baseline player so the exhibitions are tougher on him
physically than the net rushers. After he's done an exhibition tour, I noticed the
effects a month later. His legs are slow and listless and he still looks tired and
drawn.

'Sure, I know the money is tempting [Borg makes over $200,000 during a
week of exhibitions] but maybe, long-term, he could make even more if he
planned his schedule more sensibly. For example, allow one day of travel and
one day of rest before and after every exhibition. I'm just afraid he'll burn his
body up the way he's going now.

'I should go to the exhibitions too. Bjorn doesn't want to lose to McEnroe
even in an exhibition because there will be a carry over effect against John in
tournaments. He must try to be in his best shape even for exhibitions. They
should be scheduled carefully. Not this one-after-another, no rest, travel all
day, and play all night sort of thing. If someone beats you a few times even in
practice, it's easy for him to lose respect for you.'

Gene Scott: Exhibitions have been a problem for more than
just the coaches. The International Pro Council

which runs the men's tour has tried to eliminate
the big money exhibitions for years without
success. The Council's view is that these special
events dilute the fields of all Grand Prix
tournaments, which are the game's backbone.
They see a proliferation of exhibitions as
potentially destructive of the tournament concept
because if a superstar can make a million dollars
playing ten weeks of exhibitions, he'll only play
Wimbledon and the US Open and skip the rest of
the circuit. The Council has been successful in
limiting the number of exhibition weeks to six
during the periods when $175,000 or more in
prize money is offered, but fear that more
restrictions would run foul of American anti-trust
laws.

There are many theories about how much
tennis a professional athlete can manage in a year,
without affecting his peformance. If you play too
much you get stale and risk injury, too little and
you're not match tough and risk injury from not
being in shape. What constitutes too much and
too little competition is the core of the debate,
although there is general agreement that there are
too many tournaments and that the pros tend to
play too much. The reason is simple. Even when a
pro is tired after six weeks of tournaments in a
row, if a promoter offers an extra-large payday,
either for a tournament or exhibition the next
week, the temptation is tough to resist.

The ATP (player's union) is always trying to
establish new events around the world in order to
create more 'jobs' for its membership, which adds
to the lure of staying on the tour 'just one more
week'.

Complicating the question is the fact that no
two players' schedule should be the same. Some
need work to be effective, some get stale if they
play two weeks in a row. Adding more confusion
to the equation is that most players and coaches

plan their year at least six months in advance, slotting rest periods carefully into the tournament calendar. But they can't possibly predict how well they're going to perform half a year in advance. What happens if they have planned a month of tournaments and then two weeks of rest and run a bad patch of luck (poor draws, injury) or play badly and lose in an early round? Suddenly they're faced with two weeks of rest without having played more than a handful of matches. The solution is difficult because the pros must sign up for events at least forty-two days in advance, which does not allow for slumps, or the opposite, like reaching the finals three weeks in a row and wanting a rest week earlier than planned. The rules don't allow for withdrawals at all, unless injured.

In trying to find what the best schedule is for my own head and body, I announced at the 1980 Masters, that I am going to cut down playing in 1980 to ten tournaments and six weeks of exhibitions, and see how my record is. My goal this year is the same as my career goal – to win as many major titles (French, US Open, Wimbledon) as I can before I retire. It may be that by playing so little I won't be competitively sharp enough to play well in the 'majors'. If that is the case, I'll simply adjust my schedule to play more events in 1981.

Already there is enormous variety in the number of tournaments the pros play. For example, in 1979, David Schneider, Kim Warwick, Tim Wilkison, and Ray Moore played the most Grand Prix tournaments, twenty-nine each. The ones who played the fewest were myself with sixteen and Connors fifteen. But the bare statistics can be misleading. John McEnroe played twenty-one tournaments but he won seven singles events, fourteen doubles and six Davis Cup matches for a total of almost 200 matches, not including exhibitions, in the year. Clearly he played more tennis than Schneider, who lost in the early rounds in most cities he travelled to. Indeed McEnroe may have played more matches in 1979 than any player in history – certainly more than the barnstorming days of Don Budge, Jack Kramer, Bobby Riggs, and Pancho Gonzales. McEnroe thrives on working hard, possibly because he didn't play that much during his junior years, but even Mighty Mac is showing signs of cutting down his schedule significantly.

Gene Scott: Bjorn agrees with Bergelin about Flushing
            Meadows being a nightmare at night, but he
            doesn't agree about the exhibitions. It may be
            difficult for Bjorn to be objective on the issue.
            He's young enough to feel his body is immortal and
            he wants to put away as much money as possible
            before retiring.

            So while Bergelin winces whenever he first sees
            Borg come off a seven-day run of non-stop
            exhibitions, he never lets his frustration interfere
            with putting his charge in top shape, including
            daily massage by himself.

'You know the Swedes are famous for their massage technique,' Lennart says, 'and although I haven't formally been to their schools, I have been taught by some of the best masseurs in Sweden. I have been working with Bjorn's body for so long that I know it better than the local masseur in each city who sees Bjorn for the first time. His legs are my primary concern now. He has problems from time to time with his hamstring and groin. It looks as if he's at last over that terrible stomach pull during the 1976 Wimbledon. We know it came from learning the new serve which required more power and more body turn. We were very frightened then – with those injections and everything – and very lucky to win.'

Gene Scott: Borg's relationship with Bergelin is more reliance
            than dependence. Bergelin combines the roles of
            father, brother, and companion without the
            tension that is likely in family closeness. Borg
            confirms his confidence and loyalty to Bergelin
            succinctly.

As long as I play tennis and want to win, I will have Lennart around. Although Lennart doesn't travel with me all year round he comes to every big tournament, meaning his year ends after the US Open in September and starts with the Masters the following January. I can play without him, for sure, and won $180,000, the largest singles purse in tennis history, at the 1979 Montreal WCT Challenge Cup. But this was not one of the tour's major titles. For these I need Lennart. He arranges absolutely everything so I can concentrate a hundred per cent on tennis. He fixes my travel, my meal times, my practice schedule, finds practice partners, even wakes me up – everything.

In return, I pay all his travel expenses, meals, and hotel bills, plus a generous salary. In addition, he gives clinics and exhibitions himself, and endorses a clothing line. He also gets paid to work with the Swedish Davis Cup team. A lot of parents, officials, and players have asked him to take on additional coaching assignments, but so far he has refused saying that he thinks it's a full time job looking after me.

If you imagine the details involved in managing a singles tennis star are glamorous and simple, you're wrong. For instance, I hate to think of all the time Lennart spends on just one small part of my tennis existence – my tennis rackets. How many of you have ever considered that a club player is unbelievably cocky when he brings two rackets on court? And if he carries three, that he's a real hot dog?

Last year in the French Championships, I broke the strings on sixty rackets in two weeks. Sixty! In the 1975 WCT event in San Paulo I went through twenty-eight rackets in six days. My rackets are strung at eighty pounds pressure, weight fourteen and a half ounces and have a $4\frac{5}{8}$ grip. I play with Donnay world-wide, though until this year I played with the Bancroft frame in Japan, Canada and the United States.

Silhouetted on my racket strings is a large B, which most spectators thought stood for my name but really was an advertisement for the Bancroft racket I then used. Silhouetting is a clever device by manufacturers to advertise their product far more prominently than the small label on the frame, which can't even be seen by the front row of fans. With my special stringing requirement, it is a nightmare to prepare enough rackets for each tournament. There is now only one stringer in the world I allow near my rackets, Mats Laftman who lives in Stockholm. It takes a unique understanding of the delicacy of racket frames to find a pro who can even stretch eighty pounds of tension in a tennis racket without breaking the string in the process, or twisting the frame like a pretzel, let alone do it to my liking. Until recently we also had an American, Mark Williams, a pro at Jason Smith's Lincoln Plaza Racquet Club in New York, do some stringing. Once Mark was out of town and Jason himself was nice enough to try, but Lennart 'pinged' the rackets and could tell right away that a switch had been made. Lennart doesn't ever again want to worry about substitute stringers, so it's Mats exclusively now.

As a result, the procedure for keeping me in enough rackets, each tuned with the same care as for the pitch of a violin, is a giant headache.

It means every time I travel to America and back to Europe I must stop in Copenhagen to leave off at least twenty rackets for delivery to Stockholm via SAS, and pick up a fresh twenty for my next tournament. Complicating the matter further is that frequently Lennart is woken in the middle of the night by a high pitched popping noise which means a string has snapped. Lennart has to get up and sort through the entire batch of rackets to remove the single set of broken strings so the racket won't warp. The rackets can never be kept near the sun during the day nor near the air conditioner at night, or the pinging will be a symphony of strings snapping. Even if I haven't used a racket for two weeks, I will cut out the gut before a match so a fresh string can be put in.

Before 1976, Lennart used to scout players, but now we never do. If I don't know how a player plays by now, I'll never know. I think it's a lot of nonsense the way some coaches keep charts on opponents – 'sixty-four per cent of the time Newcombe hits his passing shots down the line', so on a big point you cover down the line and he hits cross-court instead. Then you're mad at both yourself and your coach.

When I was a lot younger Lennart gave me advice on strokes and strategy but in the last five years he's more like a father. There's not so much advice now. I just want to see him around. I know how to play. We never have deep discussions about tennis because he knows that I know what to do.

Gene Scott: Some critics ask why Lennart hasn't coached Bjorn to volley, for despite his being number one in the world, he has got there without learning to be aggressive at net. If you watch the Australians, John Alexander, Phil Dent, Geoff Masters, and Mark Edmonson, although none come close to Borg's overall ability, every one is a superior volleyer.

'It's difficult to tamper with success', Lennart responds. 'Tiriac is trying to make Vilas a volleyer and an all-court player. It hasn't worked. Vilas won more matches on fast surfaces by staying back than by trying to volley. It's a difficult question, whether to change the style of someone who has been comfortable in the backcourt for fifteen years. Suddenly you say he must now volley two points a game. You might destroy his effectiveness and rhythm. Coming to net when you're not used to it is like being at the frontier. You're fighting the unknown.

'The character of the player is important in determining his style, his strategy. Tiriac is trying to make Vilas a volleyer when he isn't at home at net. Vilas won the Masters in 1974 on the Melbourne grass over Nastase and Newcombe which was a great accomplishment. But what people don't realize is that he did it from the baseline. Connors and Borg have had great success on grass from the backcourt too. You must be very careful and patient if you're going to tinker with a man's style. You can't make gold out of clay. The toughest thing for a coach is to find what individual technique is best for this or that student. Everyone is different,' Bergelin concedes.

'Two years ago, two Swedes reached the US Open Junior finals, but they won't sacrifice what's necessary. They have to travel, leave home and get tournament-tough, then you look at them and the ones who don't adapt quickly, you send home. If they're unhappy with the life, don't force it. Some get homesick. You'll find out quickly. Bjorn left home and school early, and loved it. He loved his parents, yet wasn't always yearning to get home.

'Bjorn practises like he plays. He takes it very seriously. A lot of kids joke around in practice. Not Bjorn. He may just hit for an hour and a half with Gerulaitis before they begin to play sets. If they can learn to concentrate in practice where it doesn't count, think how strong their will is when a match comes.

'Tennis is a game of concentration. Was it good for Vilas for Tiriac to talk to him so much during the 1977 WCT Dallas Finals against Borg, where Tiriac would say something after every point?'

I didn't care. If you're a good player with experience you know what to do. If you're in trouble, you know how to change. A hundred per cent of my game is instinct. I never stop and think I'm going to hit a ball cross-court or down the line. I just do it.

Gene Scott: Martin, who is Borg's frequent practice partner, visited Bjorn's Swedish Island Kattilo, four hours south and east of Stockholm, to train after last summer's post-Wimbledon layoff. Kattilo is a dream retreat for a sportsman who cherishes his privacy, and is actually one large island with a main house and five small cottages, plus eleven other islands with no buildings, and none permitted by Swedish law. There is one plexipave court adjacent to the main house and that became Martin and Borg's rock pile for four hours a day for a week.

'There wasn't enough excitement on the island for me', Martin recalled, 'but that's what made it such a perfect place to practise. Lennart made sure there were enough balls, water and towels. We had no excuses to leave the court even for five minutes. The conditions were perfectly controlled for training.

'I couldn't live like he does. I need to be around people. He likes to be alone. One thing about his island, he can get mad there and no one sees him. When we practised he smashed two rackets and screamed as loud as I did. Then he'd break up laughing. He could let everything that was inside spill out and wasn't afraid of anyone judging him.

'Practising with Borg makes me a better player. He's so steady that we can practise for thirty minutes and he won't miss a ball which makes me try even harder. He doesn't need to do drills because his rallies are like two on ones.

'One reason he rarely misses is that he has a simple game. It's not based on complex patterns or strokes. He just plays regardless of his opponent's style. But I tell you, he would not be the same player without Bergelin. Lennart's combination of former great player and a "father" is rare. It's not the same with Vilas and Tiriac. It kills Lennart if Borg loses. You get the feeling Lennart is playing Borg's matches too. I'm sure Lennart cares more about his relationship with Borg than he does for his own family. I don't mean that Lennart doesn't love his wife and three kids, but Bjorn has become another son who needs Lennart six months of the year.

'Bergelin doesn't teach technique except he did help Borg with his serve in 1976. One of Bergelin's most critical functions is that he makes Borg relax – he knows exactly when it's time to work, and when it's time to laugh and forget about tennis or a bad loss. The hardest thing for most players is not to worry about the next match. Bergelin prepared everything so perfectly beforehand that Bjorn doesn't have a chance to worry.'

Gene Scott: Fred Stolle, the former Wimbledon and US Doubles titleholder is now a top teaching pro in Miami Beach, Florida. He is also Vitas Gerulaitis's coach. Not full time, but whenever a big tournament approaches, he is summoned to set the proper tone for a Championship tune-up. Like a drill sergeant, Stolle harnesses Vitas's well known off-court energy to a stern regimen of discipline. Vitas remains at home with his mother, father, and sister Ruta for ten days before any crucial event in New York City. The late night boogie at Studio 54, Xenon, and the Mudd Club is replaced by four hours of intensive training a day with plenty of rest – Vitas can sleep from 10 p.m. to noon without stirring the bedcovers an inch. One of Stolle's important tasks is to neutralize Vitas's entourage of friends. Gerulaitis is like a firefly and attracts dozens of wellwishers wherever he travels, and if it were left to Vitas, he would be having lunch or dinner with every one of them the day before the US Open.

Stolle changed that three years ago when he came to Vitas's house in King Point and discovered two friends bunking in the Gerulaitis household right before Flushing Meadows and expecting to stay the entire two weeks. Stolle threw them out.

Fred protects Vitas much in the same way Lennart protects Borg. It is difficult for either to go out for dinner without being hounded for autographs. Their simple rule is no signing until the meal is finished.

Some might question the value of Stolle, or any coach, when Gerulaitis has lost to Borg sixteen times in a row, without ever winning. But the other side of the coin is that Vitas had never beaten McEnroe and Connors in seven years and suddenly, in the course of fifteen hours during the 1980 Masters in Madison Square Garden, he defeated both, with Stolle by his side. Is a coach necessary? Stolle thinks so.

'A coach can't help much on tactics while sitting on the sideline. Even if he were able to signal his man, it wouldn't be worth more than a couple of points a match. But those points might mean the difference between winning and losing. Since I can't help Vitas while he's on court, I do want to pick up enough about his game and his opponents to offer just a few hints that could help him in a match. My advice may not help against Borg. Our strategy has never varied against Bjorn over the years. Vitas must attack his second serve, move to net, and knock off the volley. Obviously, we haven't been successful yet.

'But against other players, it's different. Ten years ago, only a half dozen guys at a tournament could beat you. Now the depth is so extraordinary that anyone in the top hundred can pull an upset. The reason is the pros are practising so hard. It used to be that Roy Emerson and Brian Gottfried were the only guys on the circuit who would practise five hours a day. Now the whole tour practises all day to try to break into the top ten.

'With these eager beavers, I can help Vitas's game plan by scouting rival

Fred Stolle, former US Singles Champion and currently Vitas Gerulaitis's coach

weaknesses and strengths beforehand. But the main quality necessary in a coach is not his tennis brain. There are dozens of experts who can spot the same things I can. The important element is respect. Vitas has got to respect me when I tell him he can't stay out all night anymore. After the tournament I know he's going to waste himself a bit. I can't be his watch dog all year long. But if he won't pay the price when I'm in town, I'll quit. He knows that.

'Ironically, we know how to beat Borgie. Attack. McEnroe handles him best – hits that lefty serve wide to the backhand and comes in on his forehand. We've tried everything. Staying back, coming in on shots down the middle. Nothing has worked because Vitas's style fits right into Borg's strength. You know they practise all the time together, and some points they play are the best I've ever seen. When they start to practise with six balls, they're so steady and fast they won't get to use the third ball for twenty minutes. Often Vitas kills Bjorn in practice. I think the difference is that Vistas serves much better in practice and Bjorn rarely serves flat out until a match. Mentally Borg is something else. To win Wimbledon for four years without coming to net is one hell of an effort!'

5. Wimbledon

Wimbledon has a special flavour for me. For many it is a gathering of flowered hats and flower pots, of strawberries and cream and champagne, and a grizzly hotdog called an Oscar. Wimbledon is a celebration more than anything else. Spectators ignore contradictions such as the parking costing more than admission to the grounds. Ninety per cent of the matches in the first week are played on field courts where there is no reserved seating. First come first served – on park benches mostly, except that there is a small cement stadium on Courts Two and Three, and at the south diagonal of the grounds sits Court Fourteen with over a thousand seats rising seventy feet straight up along the east tram line. But the world has only heard of the Centre Court, which seats twelve thousand, with standing room for another three thousand. This is less than half the number of fans Wimbledon admits every day. An attendance of 34,000 is not unusual per day, and in 1979 a record 343,044 people came to watch over the fortnight. Where do they all fit? Seven thousand fit in a mirror image of the Centre Court, Court Number One. The three small field stands accommodate another five thousand and everyone else just mills about. It is not an unusual sight to see four thousand people standing outside the Centre Court waiting for nothing in particular to happen – just standing in the English sun (when it comes out).

I love the English. They are so serious about their tennis and everything else too. Tradition is God here. All matches start 'at 2 p.m. precisely', even if there is a rain delay. The British always act so totally surprised when it rains, as if a downpour is as rare as snow in the Caribbean. All players must wear predominantly white and we may not practise on the grounds during the fortnight unless we are scheduled for the Centre Court or Court Number One.

Class distinctions do exist for the players despite Wimbledon's attempts to see to it that all competitors are treated equally. It is true that the pro ranked 128 will be given the same as the number one seed: one tea and luncheon ticket per day, limousine service to and from his hotel in London fifteen miles away, and full practice facilities at the

Queens Club ten miles away from Wimbledon; but it is also true that there is an A and B locker room with all the stars residing in A. Furthermore, if you win the Mens or Ladies Singles, you are made a full member of the All England Club with precious rights to two Centre Court seats each day.

The Wimbledon Championship, to insiders, is simply called the Championships – as if no other tournament in the world existed. I feel the same way about it, and not because the facilities are that great – they're not. The locker room is small and overcrowded, and the lockers themselves are wooden, ten inches by thirty inches, and too small for street clothes which must be hung on bench hooks. There are too few showers and the streams from the small nozzle heads hit you with blasts of water that feel like sleet on your back. And it does rain a lot in London, making practice impossible. Still, there is nothing like the Centre Court for a final. The committee makes you feel that nothing is more important, and their organisation has framed a perfect place for a championship match.

In the beginning I was not so sure I could ever play well on grass. After all, before 1976 my record was not very impressive. In 1973, the year all the ATP players boycotted Wimbledon because the ITF banned Nikki Pilic for not playing Davis Cup, I lost to Roger Taylor in the quarter-finals and the next year I was killed by Ismail El Shafei in the third round 6-2, 6-3, 6-1. In 1975, I lost to Arthur Ashe (the eventual Champion) in the quarter-finals 2-6, 6-4, 8-6, 6-1.

I had a good chance to go to the finals that year. If I hadn't had a leg injury I might have beaten Ashe, then Tony Roche, who was past his peak, in the semi-finals. I might have lost to Connors in the final but, either way, I was building confidence on grass. I had won my first grass court tournament in 1974 over Onny Parun in the New Zealand Open and this convinced me that even without volleying I could win on grass.

My only early success at Wimbledon was in 1972 when, at sixteen, I won the Juniors, hardly an earthshaking event, except that I did manage to enrage Buster Mottram who was leading in the final set 5-2 before I ran off five straight games and the match 7-5. But until twenty I was considered a good slow court player without a volley and totally unsuited for the lightning pitch at Wimbledon. Furthermore, the international calendar is so peculiar that it schedules the French Championships, the unofficial world clay court title, to end just two weeks before Wimbledon begins. The adjustment from clay to grass is

Ever since 1973 I've had to have a regular escort at Wimbledon to protect me from over-admiring teenagers

too difficult to make in just two weeks. If you don't believe it, take a look at the record. Only two players in the past twenty-three years have won the French and Wimbledon the same year, Rod Laver and myself.

The last four years that I have won Wimbledon, my practice routine has been virtually identical every day. After Paris I rest for three days; no tennis, just sleep and eat. The French tournament is so tiring, physically and mentally, I don't want to see a tennis ball. Lennart, Mariana and I stay in Hampstead, in a large suite at the Holiday Inn with two bedrooms, a kitchenette and a living room. It is forty-five minutes from Wimbledon but it is worth the drive to be totally isolated for the world's most important Championship. Two minutes away from the Hotel is the Cumberland Lawn Tennis and Cricket Club where I practise every day for four hours, two hours in the morning, two hours in the afternoon, with my regular practice partners, Heinz Gunthardt, Billy Martin, and Vitas Gerulaitis. The Cumberland Club wrote in February 1980 for an increased fee of $900 each for me and Vitas for the two weeks of practice. We need the practice but we also give a free exhibition for the members which we'd charge $50,000 for in another country. I asked Bob Kain to offer what we paid the year before.

The reason I don't spend long at Wimbledon is that they make it so difficult to practise. Technically, you're allowed only half an hour of practice a day the week before Wimbledon begins. Virtually every player ignores the rule and shares 'half hours' with as many players as he can find. But it's still a hassle running from court to court so you don't waste a precious minute of sign-up time. As a former Champion, I am accorded special playing privileges two weeks before the event, but often the courts are closed for maintenance or rain, so it seems better to be off on our own.

Some of my personal rituals are trivial but we observe them with a smile just the same. For example SAAB, as part of my contract, gives me a car in every city I visit. For Wimbledon the car must have a radio. In 1979, it didn't and Lennart was so superstitious he turned the car in for one with a full blast stereo. Another ritual we observe is that Lennart always drives and I sit in the front seat with Mariana in the back. Most of the time Mariana cooks all our meals, occasionally we go out to a restaurant or for a movie, but not often. For breakfast she cooks bacon and eggs, and we have cornflakes, coffee, and orange juice; nothing heavy for lunch because we practise afterwards: cheese, cold ham or chicken, milk or squash; for dinner, steaks and fish, or sometimes Mariana prepares a special Romanian dish of chicken and peas with a spicy sauce. I make sure my weight stays around 160 lbs.

'He's crazy about his weight', Mariana says. 'If he puts on two pounds in Monte Carlo during a rest period, he'll put on his track suit and jog a hundred laps around our garden. He's also very superstitious. His parents alternate years they come to Wimbledon and Paris. This year they won't visit Wimbledon but will watch at Paris. Next year, vice versa until the streak is broken.'

My training during this period never consists of running. Maybe I am not always in tune mentally but after two weeks on clay in Paris, I am in shape physically. We get up at 9 a.m. and after breakfast we are on the practice court by ten, where I rally for forty-five minutes or so. No drills, no set routine of forehands, then backhands, just rally. Actually, the first week, we may hit even longer just to get a feel of the ball on grass. I hate drills. They're boring. I haven't drilled for five years.

'Borg doesn't have to drill formally – his rallying *is* a drill because often he doesn't miss a ball for stretches of ten minutes at a time.'
Vitas Gerulaitis

After warming up, Vitas or Billy and I will play four or five sets in the morning and another four or five sets in the afternoon. The Club orders a gross of Slazenger balls in advance for our preparation. We give special attention to return of serve, which I think is the most important stroke at Wimbledon. You have to serve well, but most of the contenders already have good serves and believe me, the difference between winning and losing at the Championships is return of serve.

One of the nice things about the Cumberland Club is that they will let us play on a wet court. Wimbledon shuts down the grass for practice at the first drop so the turf isn't damaged. When it really floods down, we practise indoors at the London Vanderbilt Club which is owned by an eccentric Hungarian, Geza Gazdag, who pioneered indoor tennis in New York City with his first Vanderbilt facility.

The only variation from this ritual was in 1976 when I practised serving for hours. Both Lennart and I felt that too many players were taking advantage of my second serve and that my first was neither forceful nor accurate enough. The intensive work on the overall service motion was the most productive training I've had in the past five years – because it worked.

People ask why I don't play doubles any more. There is a very good reason. The last time I played doubles in an important tournament other than Davis Cup, where I have to play, was at Wimbledon 1976. I played with Vilas and, during a late afternoon match, I tore a stomach muscle, already sore from too much serving, and was almost forced to default from the singles. But Lennart found a doctor who said that with injections every day I might continue. When I beat Vilas 6-3, 6-0, 6-2 in the quarter-finals I knew the pain killers worked, but I didn't consider what long-term damage they might do. For six days, an hour before each match, I received three injections in my stomach which numbed my hips, side, stomach, and even part of my legs for six hours. I not only survived, I didn't lose a set in the tournament but when I went into training for Davis Cup after a three week vacation, my stomach muscles were still destroyed. I couldn't lift my arm above my head to serve without pain and withdrew from the team for an even longer rest period. The next serious tennis I played that year was two months later at the US Open.

I do like doubles, but if you're trying to do well in the singles, it just doesn't make sense to play the team event. The matches are always scheduled at the end of the day after you've played a hard singles and when you're most vulnerable to injury. At Wimbledon, they often play on the Centre Court until 9 p.m. when it's usually cold and dank. The problem is you may be on again the next day at 2 p.m. for a crucial singles match.

In 1978, the day before Gerulaitis had to play Connors in the semi-finals, he had to play two doubles matches, the round of sixteen and the quarter-finals, both of which went to five sets. He didn't leave the club grounds until 9 p.m. and went out to Connors the next day in sixty-five minutes 9-7, 6-2, 6-1. Vitas was a wreck against Connors, not that he wasn't in shape – Vitas is always in shape – but that competitive edge had been dulled by staying out on a doubles court for six hours the day before.

Of the top six, Vilas, Connors, Gerulaitis, and myself never play doubles, Tanner plays but without much success. McEnroe is the best doubles player in the world and he feels it helps his singles, but that's for two reasons. John doesn't like to practise and the doubles gives him more court time which the rest of us get in practice. Besides, he's young, energetic, and strong enough to carry the extra strain that doubles puts on you.

I think I could play good doubles because I return serve well. But I would have to play all the time. Right now, the few times I play in Davis Cup and exhibitions I have no confidence because the angles and strategy are so different. But I'd be crazy ever to play the doubles at Wimbledon as long as I care about winning the singles.

I think my best Wimbledon tennis was in 1976 when I won without losing a set. I was not supposed to win so there was no pressure. I just hit away in each match and it seemed impossible to miss. I still didn't have much experience on grass, no really big wins, and my serve was still suspect. But I thought I had a chance. First I saw the semi-finals as a definite possibility. Then, once I made the finals, I knew it would be difficult even though it was Nastase, against whom I felt confident. But he had been in a Wimbledon final before, and I was worried about his experience. I remember losing the first three games and being scared I wouldn't win a game and would be the first person ever to lose a Wimbledon final, 6-0, 6-0, 6-0. Then after I won a few games I relaxed. I reached the stage where the score was reasonably close and I hadn't embarrassed myself. I had already done well to get to the finals, and now I had nothing to lose. Then I started playing well, hitting lines and returning everything with no pressure.

That was also the year Mariana and I became close. She had been staying at another smaller hotel, but a few days before the Championships I asked her why she didn't move into Lennart's and my suite at the Grosvenor House. When I first asked Lennart, he wasn't pleased but said OK. Mariana moved in the next day which made me happy and relaxed.

1977 was physically the most punishing Wimbledon ever for me. I barely won against Mark Edmonson in a second round five-setter on the new Court Fourteen. The surface was soft, and there was no way we could have any rallies. I was playing OK but the ball just didn't bounce. Even Ilie Nastase had problems with this court. After he polished off Eliot Teltscher 6-4, 6-3, 6-1, mobs of teenagers surrounded him pushing over the barriers and causing serious concern about crowd control and the safety of the alleyways. Nastase had a major role in preventing what could have been a catastrophe by exercising patience and humour with his worshippers. Afterwards in the tea room Nastase asked, 'Why do all these little girls like me? I'm thirty-one, married and very ugly.'

I had some rough patches with Nikki Pilic's savage left-handed serve but won 9-7, 7-5, 6-3 in the third round. The next test was against Gerulaitis in a semi-final that British commentator Dan Maskell called 'one of the best matches ever seen on the Centre Court – in the same family as the 1972 Smith-Nastase final.' It lasted over three hours and each time I'd get a tiny lead Vitas would charge to catch up.

I thought I was going to lose when he got a break in the fifth set. He was playing unbelievably well and I got tired, though I think he was tired too. I remember thinking, if I lose it's because this guy has just played too well for too long. The biggest point of the match was when Vitas stayed back on his second serve at 40-30, leading 3-2 in games. Up to that point he had come to net on anything. We had a long rally and finally he came in. I passed him with a backhand down the line.

After I broke back, I killed him with two lucky topspin lobs, one that caught him off balance forcing him to hit an awkward overhead wide and the other that tricked him totally – he could only watch helplessly from the net as the ball soared over his head.

If I had lost the 1977 final, I would have killed myself. I had 4-0 and 30-40 for 5-0 in the fifth set against Connors. When he came back to four all, the feeling I had was unbelievable. I almost started to cry. It's a Wimbledon final, you had the match won and now you've lost it. I've never had that feeling before or since. Even my five-setters against Edmonson and Gerulaitis were not as harrowing.

I started the Connors match exhausted because of that long semi-final with Gerulaitis. I had been playing team tennis with Cleveland and was tired generally from all the travelling. To get up for another day right after Vitas was tough. Connors is like me, he hates to lose. You always feel the pressure against Jimmy. He is trying like hell and it's a great feeling to beat him because you know he's tried so hard on every point. He always puts out his best. I lost the first set 6-3 and won the next two very easily. Then at four-all in the fourth I had break point for 5-4, my serve to follow for the match. I played a bad point and lost it, and the set 7-5. A poor point does affect me though I try not to let it. But I sense the disappointment. After a short while I convince myself that thinking about the past won't help. I can block out the missed point, but not right away.

Overall I think officials are pretty good. I get angry over bad calls but, during a long match, the standard is OK. I don't lose confidence in the umpires, though I know many players do. The only real solution is to do something electronically with the lines, and a secret device is being made in Sweden. There's a court hidden by technicians in a forest in the south of Sweden where all the lines are wired. The umpire has earphones so he alone can hear when a ball is in or out. At

The trophy after my 1977 Wimbledon. No words are necessary (opposite)

Wimbledon, it's a tradition that you have to be old to be a Centre Court linesman. And they never change their minds.

When I was ahead 4-0 and a point for 5-0 in the final set, I remember getting tentative. It was as if I wanted Jimmy to lose the point rather than to win it myself. I lost depth on my groundstrokes and missed far too many first serves. Connors, sensing my hesitation, was suddenly all over the court smacking returns and approaches for winners. His serve had new bite and quickly he came back to four-all. But it is far easier to take risks and play boldly when you are behind. As soon as he had caught up, he lost his daring. He double faulted on the first point at four-all, and became timid. I won seven of the last eight points. It was the tiredest tennis match I have ever played. After three and a half hours on the Centre Court, I couldn't have played another game.

'Borg may appear calm or tired on the surface, but underneath there is still fire. He's tougher mentally and physically than Connors.'
Lennart Bergelin

1978 was a strange final. Jimmy started out so well. That year I was under a lot of pressure and was nervous because I had a chance to win Wimbledon a third time. Yet, at the same time, I was more relaxed than the first year I won. Victor Amaya was my major stumbling point in 1978. I hate playing first rounds. Everything is strange, the courts, the weather, the grounds, the crowds, the scene. It takes almost a week to get used to. There were no bounces and no rallies (and no sunshine even – it was 52°F) for five sets against Amaya. He had me two sets to one, 3-1 and break point on my second serve in the fourth. Here my philosophy of taking chances when you're behind paid off. I cracked a hard serve down the middle, Victor was totally taken by surprise and fell apart. I won the last two sets 6-3, 6-3.

Unlike any other major tournament you can't ever practise on Wimbledon's Centre Court. At the French, US, and Australian Open, you can always hit a few on the stadium court to get used to the surroundings. But at Wimbledon you can't hit one single ball on the Centre Court. I'm used to practising on the same, or a similar, court before I play my first round match – that's why first rounds are so difficult for me at Wimbledon. Also the grass is slick and soft the first week. By the second Monday, the turf is worn down and playing more like a clay court.

I wasn't that confident I would win in 1978 against Connors, yet I

Connors and I give traditional bows to the Royal Box after my victory in the 1978 Wimbledon Final. Even without the scoreboard, Jimmy's expression tells the story (above)   (*Credit: Art Seitz*)

Here I am with Fred Perry, Wimbledon Champion 1934–6, whose record I broke with my fourth Wimbledon title in 1979 (below)   (*Credit: Art Seitz*)

wasn't really worried that I would lose. One thing helped. Jimmy can't hurt me on his serve. His first serve doesn't go in as often as during his big year, 1974, and it's not as hard. If you serve well on grass, you can win easy points, stupid points, free points because uneven bounces make it difficult to return. Also, when I have to volley I know the grass will help because the ball won't sit up. A short bad volley is good on grass.

The scores, 6-2, 6-2, 6-3, suggest I destroyed Jimmy. He won the first two games and only five afterwards, but the tennis from both of us was good. It's just that I won every single big point. And for the first time I came to net much of the time, missing only one volley in the entire match.

Gene Scott: Fred Perry, the last player to win three Wimbledons in a row, and never one known to be kind about the achievements of the game's modern men, said to the press after Borg had tied with his record, 'No player in history could have lived on Centre Court with Bjorn today. Connors is a great player but he got steamrolled.'

At Wimbledon, the post match interviews are taped, edited, and typed for distribution to those members of the press who were watching other matches. The following are the transcripts round by round of Borg's record breaking 1979 Wimbledon.

Wimbledon – First Round
Monday 25 June 1979
Bjorn Borg versus Tom Gorman   Borg won: 3-6, 6-4, 7-5, 6-1
Duration of match: 2 hours 6 minutes

It was the same sort of match as last year against Amaya. This time it was four sets; last year it was five. If Gorman had been lucky he could have won in three straight sets. When I was down 15-40 in the first game of the second set, it was important to win that game. At the start Gorman served well but I returned better as the match went on. I was nervous and tight but that was because it was the first match. It was a bit difficult to move on the wet court, but after the rain stopped totally it was much better.

There was some controversy after one of my backhands zoomed

crazily off the frame for a winner in what three years ago would have been called an illegal double hit. But the rule now is that as long as the stroke is one continuous motion, and not 'carried' on purpose, the double hit is permitted.

The first couple of rounds are the most difficult, for everyone has to get used to the grass, the balls and other things. I don't think I played very well today, but I was satisfied to win. I have been practising four to five hours each day. I worked hard and felt in good shape.

Wimbledon – Second Round
Wednesday 27 June 1979
Bjorn Borg versus Vijay Amritraj   Borg won: 2-6, 6-4, 4-6, 7-6, 6-2
Duration of match: 2 hours 46 minutes

I felt I had definitely lost the match at 3-1 and also at 0-40, 3-2, fourth set. I was relieved to win that set in the tie-breaker and by then was playing well. Vijay became very nervous in the tie-break for he made two weak shots. He was especially good when ahead and winning. It was almost exactly the same as last year against Amaya when I was 3-1 down in the fourth set. But I didn't think about last year. I have been down like this before. I am more relaxed when I'm behind and go all out to play winners. Some of the time I do it. I was not nervous at all. Still there's no way I can keep winning. I have to lose sometimes. No one can win every single match in every single tournament.

Today's game was even closer than against Amaya last year. I've had two tight matches so far and now face Pfister. I've had service problems but I'm not worried. It can come right any day. I pulled something in my leg against Gorman but I hope it will be better with a day's rest tomorrow. I have played Pfister twice before and won twice; they were both tight.

This is the toughest draw I've ever had at Wimbledon. I know Pfister likes to play on grass and he must have played very well to beat Peter Fleming in four sets. He has a big serve but I am confident of being able to return it if I play well.

Wimbledon – Third Round
Friday 29 June 1979
Bjorn Borg versus Hank Pfister   Borg won: 6-4, 6-1, 6-3
Duration of match: 1 hour 12 minutes

I didn't feel my injury much today except when I had to reach wide on the forehand or backhand. I pulled a hamstring at the back of my left thigh but if it is like this for my next match, I'll be satisfied. Whatever happens, if I am going to lose it will be on the tennis court – not off it. I have been having ice treatment on the injury every day, also ultra-sonic and cream massage. Before today's match I had some hot stuff rubbed on. Yesterday I rested as much as possible and just had one hour hitting. I have not been pretending about my injury. The treatment I have had has made a difference and I am just going to see how I feel tomorrow.

The doctor says the best treatment is rest. I am not going to have any injections. I was a little scared at the beginning not knowing how my injury would react but I felt better and better as the game went on. My return of serve was very good today and it was my best match against Pfister so far. He missed many first serves and he has played better. Even if I lose this year I will come back to Wimbledon and play next year.

Wimbledon – Round of Sixteen

Saturday 30 June 1979
Bjorn Borg versus Brian Teacher   Borg won 6-4, 5-7, 6-4, 7-5
Duration of match: 2 hours 29 minutes

In a sense, I was ready for Teacher because he played exactly the way Pfister did in the last round. Big serve, charge the net. Even on my serve he tried to get to the net all the time. I was worried. There weren't many rallies. It was very windy on Court One today, making it difficult to control the ball. Besides you never know how well he is going to play. If he plays perfectly I'm out of the tournament. But I started to play consistently in the Pfister match so I had confidence for Teacher. I've finally got used to the conditions, the crowds and the weather.

This match was very, very close. It was one set all and it could have gone either way in the third set. I did win that one, but the fourth was even trickier. He hit a lot of first serves in, which I was returning solidly, but I still never came close to breaking serve until the end. He had a lot of chances to break me and win that last set.

For me, I was very aggressive, mixing up my play by serving and volleying, rallying a few balls and then following an approach to net. I felt I had to come in more because if I didn't, he would. It was like a race to see who could get to net first.

Wimbledon – Quarter-final

Tuesday 3 July 1979
Bjorn Borg versus Tom Okker   Borg won: 6-2, 6-1, 6-3
Duration of match: 1 hour 7 minutes

This was probably my simplest quarter-final ever at Wimbledon, but probably not my best. Tom didn't play well and missed a lot of easy volleys. I feel I am playing well. I am still having treatment on my leg but it hasn't bothered me for the last two matches and it doesn't matter if I play a long match or a sixty-seven-minute one like this. I don't feel in trouble. I believe Connors should have been seeded number 2 and it's a pity to meet Connors in the semi-final. Still, there are some good guys in the lower half, and to reach the final anyone has to play well. At the moment Connors is in good form and has improved a lot, and he is now playing with a lot of confidence and hitting the ball hard and deep. I always believe I am going to win, but against Connors I never know.

There is no way that I can play below my best and win. Tomorrow I will practise for a couple of hours and the rest of the time I will relax and get myself ready for Thursday. It's good to have a day off after a tough match but, like all players, I prefer to play every day.

It was more exciting for me in 1976 than it is this year for I never dreamed I could win then. Now everything is working out well and I am completely satisfied with my play, except possibly for my first serve. Little bothers me on court. Much of the rest time I spend in bed. There is a little more pressure on Connors now, than on me, for I have been winning lately. Earlier he was beating me more often and I was under pressure.

Wimbledon – Semi-final

Thursday 5 July 1979
Bjorn Borg versus Jimmy Connors   Borg won: 6-2, 6-3, 6-2
Duration of match: 1 hour 16 minutes

I expected a much tougher match because I did not think I would play so well today. Also Jimmy was below his best. I played as well as I did in the final last year. Jimmy didn't say anything to me after the game. He's probably in a bad temper. I would be, too, if I lost. Obviously, we are going to play many more matches against each other and I feel very confident now. He beat me seven of the first eight times we played, starting in 1973, but this has changed. I have won eight of the last eleven matches. I am hitting my groundstrokes better. Earlier in my career I played more soft balls and he put pressure on me. Now I am hitting through the ball and getting better depth on both sides. In the early days he was able to come in, but now he has to stay back.

Today, Jimmy missed a lot of first serves. In last year's final he did the same thing. I served well, especially in the first two sets. I have to, because he returns so well. This is the first match in the tournament that I have served well. He played a very good game when he broke my serve at the start of the third set, but I was still feeling good.

To me Connors is just another player. I like him as a person – I'm just not very close to him. I knew before the tournament began that the first week would be difficult. In the last three years I started playing better by the quarter-finals. It is the same this year. I feel happy about Saturday's final, whomever I play. I know some felt that the match with Connors was virtually the final, but Tanner could be more difficult for me. There are two things which I might improve, my serve and volley. I still get the same thrill and excitement about winning. I always want to win a big tournament. I have no idea why Jimmy leaves the ground so quickly after the matches and doesn't turn up at press conferences. I feel if I don't go to them I might get a bad press the next day.

Press question: **How would you play against yourself?**
Borg: **I have no idea. I wouldn't tell you anyhow.**

Wimbledon – Final
Saturday 7 July 1979
Roscoe Tanner versus Bjorn Borg   Borg won: 6-7, 6-1, 3-6, 6-3, 6-4
Duration of match: 2 hours 50 minutes

Tanner's interview. If I had won that last point it would have meant three points in a row for me but the ball kicked a bit. It was not a very bad bounce but I missed it and the title was his. My coach, Dennis Ralston, told me during the match to keep working at him, and I had to take some chances on his serve to avoid being crowded out. You have to take chances against Bjorn because he is so much better than anyone else. You have to keep him out of his groove and rhythm. I felt in places that I made some errors which could have been avoided, and he jumped on my second serve too often. At no time did I feel nervous or tense about anything. I was just going for my shots. There was no reason for nerves for there was no pressure on me and I was keyed up to win. Still, being in the final is not all that bad. I wasn't aware of the crowd noises which probably meant that I concentrated more. I think the noise implied that they were enjoying a good match.

I was not tired in any way at the end, although during the match I was a little weary after certain points. He makes you work so hard and some of his high returns mean a lot of stretching. His serve seemed to be getting weaker towards the end. I served a pretty good match even though I missed some. You have got to concede that he will occasionally break you; he is such a good player.

Tomorrow I will probably start remembering all those chances of winning I had. I have to think of ways to improve on my errors, even though I bothered him a lot today. The most important period of the match was when I led 40-15 on his serve at 3-4 down in the final set. I had a great chance of making it 4-4 and, when you come down to it, just one or two points made all the difference. Dennis had written down some strategy and during a difficult part of the match I pulled out the piece of paper, read it, started all over again, and won the next three games. For part of the match Borg seemed rather tentative, especially in the first set, perhaps because he was going for the fourth title. I think I played a good match against a very good player.

Borg's interview. I can't yet believe I have won Wimbledon for the fourth time. It hasn't sunk in yet. There will be a big celebration eventually, probably for the next three or four days. Today I feel much older than I am. I was unbelievably nervous at the end and almost couldn't hold my racket when he came back in the last game from 0-40 to deuce. If he had won that game I could never have won the match. In the beginning he was serving very well and winning the big points but later I started to take the big points. That was after I decided to come in more. I had to put pressure on him and make sure that I got the ball back and he began to make mistakes especially with his volleys. It was difficult to get the feel of the ball and the rhythm of my ground strokes because of the tricky wind, and there was no way I could lob in the conditions. I thought I would certainly lose the match when he was ahead two sets to one. I never felt in the fight because the points were over so quickly. He'd ace me or miss. I didn't control anything. Nothing was happening. Nothing worked. A couple of good points or a break can help enormously. When I get that break point I always play it safely. As soon as it was 2 sets all, I thought I had a good chance of winning, especially when I broke the first game of the fifth set. He had a lot of chances to break back, and I remember hoping each time that he would miss. I just didn't want the ball to come back.

When I won for the first time in 1976 I never imagined I could do it four times running. This is the biggest thrill of my life.

My future goal is to win more big titles and be regarded as the greatest player of all time. I have won twenty-eight matches at Wimbledon and Rod Laver has won thirty-one, so I want to go for that record next year. My next big tournament is the US Open. I will definitely play in it and I am going to get myself a hundred per cent fit. I seemed fated to win all the big points in this tournament, especially today, but there will come a time when I start losing those points. For the last three or four matches I haven't felt any trouble with my left thigh. Only at the start did it trouble me. This was the most difficult of my four finals because of the way Roscoe was serving. It was even harder than my five-set match with Connors. The pressure was on me for I knew I had to hold my serve, otherwise I would lose. It was very important to break him at the start of the fifth set. I always felt one step behind until I realized I was finally ahead in the fifth. Some people wonder why I stay back, especially on my second serve. Most opponents come in to attack it, but I have such good passing shots that I don't mind that. My parents have been here all the tournament and they have seen me win Wimbledon twice. They were also here in 1977.

During that last game when I was serving for the match, my mother was watching in the player's guest section, she always eats candy for luck when I play. She spat it out on the floor when I was 40-0 triple match point. I lost three straight points to deuce. She was so nervous she looked for the candy on the floor, found it, and popped it back in her mouth. I won the next two points and the match.

I wasn't praying to my parents as I told the press afterwards. I was kidding them. I didn't think about what I was going to do before the last point. I just did it. I'm not religious. I wasn't praying to God either. I was brought up as a Protestant but I've only been to church once in my life, when I was nine. I was curious that one time but now I don't think about religion. Sometimes I thank God. I believe, and I don't believe, in something up there. I don't understand it.

Gene Scott: To set Borg's record straight, it should be understood that other men have won four straight Wimbledons. William Renshaw won six (1881–1886); Reggie F. Doherty won four (1897–1900)

and his brother H. Laurie Doherty won five
(1902–1906); and Tony Wilding won four (1910–
1913). Wilding was the only one of these early
champions who had to play through the entire
tournament – and he did it just once – because
prior to 1913, the Champion was exempt until the
Challenge Round just like the format of the Davis
Cup before 1974. Road Laver won Wimbledon
four times with a five-year gap between the second
and third times (1961–1962, 1968–1969). He didn't
play in those intervening five years because pros
weren't permitted at Wimbledon until 1968.

6. Tennis myths

Gene Scott: The name Bjorn means 'bear' in Swedish. It
          doesn't fit Bjorn Borg. Bjorn is a cougar or an
          eagle but never so plodding an animal as a bear.
          His raw speed and acceleration are magnified by
          their effortlessness. Bjorn never appears to be
          moving quickly and yet he is never out of
          position. The fact that he rarely has to rush,
          indeed he is usually waiting correctly placed long
          before the ball reaches him, is a striking advantage
          in stroke preparation. The Swedish name Borg, on
          the other hand, means 'castle'. The perfect
          description for a player whose defence is
          impenetrable.

Breaking down tennis myths is as difficult as learning to play tennis left-handed if you're right-handed. In the days of the Puritans, when government leaders insisted there were witches, and that they were wicked and had to be burned at the stake, they were. Officials had to be right, didn't they? So, too, in tennis, myths have been offered as truth by the 'experts' with no room for questioning. There is no process whereby a tennis axiom can be tested and tossed out if times have changed, or if the 'truth' was not true in the first place. Countless tennis tips have been passed on from generation to generation without the fresh air of a new theory or any examination of the old one.

A prime problem of instruction methods is that the degree of acceptance is often directly related to the reputation of the man teaching, regardless of whether the theory is cock-eyed or not. For instance, Hall of Famer, Jack Kramer, says that on the return of serve you should hold your racket with the forehand grip and lean to the right, or forehand, side. I do exactly the opposite, holding with the backhand grip and the racket tilting all the way to the backhand.

Another juicy bit of instruction is the advice to hit the ball on the

Caricature by David Levine

rise. There is a macho urge to strike the ball immediately it comes off the ground. No one has bothered to add that while hitting on the rise is the ultimate offensive game and dramatic to watch and play, it is low percentage tennis; it's flashy but won't win consistently. I conclude that the advantages of hitting on the rise – the element of surprise and using your opponent's power – are marginal compared to the risks.

Hitting on the rise is like half volleying and I half volley only because I have to – not because I want to – where my opponent has trapped me out of position and I'm forced to flick at the ball without normal preparation. The advantages of hitting a ball at the top of its bounce, on the other hand, are obvious. The ball's direction will be from a high point to a low point over the net and down into the court rather than the necessary arc from low to high over the net. In addition, you have more time for preparation. Often, when I need more time to set up, I'll hit the ball as it's falling from the bounce rather than meeting it at the top. The added time is important to two-handers whose backswing requires more stages to put together. That is not to say that some players are not sometimes successful in hitting on the rise, including Connors, Fleming, and McEnroe, particularly on the return of serve when they are going for a one shot winner. However, the art of hitting on the rise is an imprecise science not recommended for pros or amateurs. And the concentration required to hit continually on the rise is intense, which will be tiring in a long match.

If you expect me to offer standard advice such as, 'take your racket back, follow through, and watch the ball', stop reading. I believe tennis is a game of instinct and common sense, rather than proper grips and tedious tips. Not that a youngster doesn't need the fundamentals of stroke production, but once basic guidelines have been laid down and those fundamentals have been etched on a beginner's mind by constant practice, progress from there is a state of mind rather than a state of form.

I have broken nearly every rule recommended by instruction books for the past fifty years. For example, the normal advice on where to stand when returning serve is a foot *beyond* the baseline. And when receiving a second serve – a foot *inside* the baseline. Anyone who has seen me play knows I don't do this.

Court Position for Service Return

I position myself at least ten feet past the baseline, and when Roscoe Tanner is serving, I retreat even further back. The reason? I want to get the longest look possible at a hard serve. I need ample time to sight the direction of delivery, then wind up and swing at the ball.

To me, standing at the baseline to return serve is for show-offs. Maybe a star can play a spectacular winner standing close in, but for every winner struck, he'll miss a dozen. My idea is to get every single service return back so as to pressurize the net man into missing. Because my goal is not to hit instant winners, there is no burden on me in returning serve.

Having more time to hit the ball by standing back, plus the no-pressure frame of mind, is a devastating combination. The result is that I end up hitting more outright winners on return of serve than anyone else on the pro tour. Why? The element of surprise.

Most big servers on a fast surface (the grass at Wimbledon, the asphalt at the US Open) are spoiled by being able to make thirty per cent of their first serves virtually unreturnable, meaning that thirty per cent of the time the server fires, and then relaxes. He's lulled by the flubs of players standing close to the baseline. I return every serve. This both annoys and surprises opponents. Watch the next tournament match I play against Tanner or Jimmy Connors. Many times they'll serve a ball that is normally an ace against players who return from close in and, as a result, they relax on their way to net. Midway to the service line they stand up thinking the return won't come back. But because I'm standing so far away, I have plenty of time to have a solid crack at the ball which often zips by the unprepared net man.

Why do receivers continue to stand so close in? Mostly because it's macho to face a cannonball next to the barrel, like the gladiators in the olden days chasing each other with axes or swords at close range.

Two stars – John McEnroe and Jimmy Connors – have such swift eye-to-brain-to-arm motor control that they actually see the ball coming at them sooner than other players. This phenomenal reflex capacity means that they can stand in the mouth of the cannon, so to speak, and pick up the approaching serve instantly. But even Connors, as he gets older, has started to lose this facility, leaving McEnroe as the only pro with 'radar eyes'. And McEnroe admits this ability does not help him at all in returning serve on clay, where the ball slows down enough for anyone to return it efficiently. You can add the fact that only a few fools try to serve and volley consistently on clay, and that eliminates the receiver's need to surprise the server.

As I say, the macho image has much to do with why pros and amateurs alike dig in close to the baseline to return serve. Me? I want my macho moment in the winner's enclosure rather than during a few isolated points in the match.

My advice works for beginners, too. Many amateurs crash their first serve and pitty-pat the second. I suggest standing way behind the baseline to return serve to give yourself sufficient time to take your racket back and swing, in the unlikely event of the crash serve going in. Even after a first serve fault, move in only to the point where you have ample time to prepare your stroke. Of course there is a 'give-up' in standing back. An opponent might exploit the angles of a wide serve, but the benefits of having more time, in my opinion, far outweigh the risks.

I'm not alone in my cautious philosophy of waiting for the ball far past the baseline rather than taking a bolder position right on it. Guillermo Vilas, who has one of the best clay court records in recent history, also waits patiently behind the baseline. Certainly there are some disadvantages for top pros with this style, the main one being that they have to be in extraordinary shape to execute this defensive game plan successfully. A simple study of court angles shows that you don't have to run as far if you stand in further and move along the diagonals towards the net when, in a sense, you are cutting the ball off before it becomes a punishing stroke. Also, you can use your opponent's pace more effectively if there is less distance between you and the net.

Pancho Gonzalez was one of the first proponents of manoeuvering an opponent like a puppet, while standing on the baseline tape. But Pancho hit an underspin backhand and a forehand with only moderate overspin. He was merely waiting for the first opportunity to attack.

My game is based on patience. Not attack. But my topspin drives prevent foes attacking because I have enough control to shoot my groundstrokes from side to side. If an opponent decides to come to net behind less than a perfect approach, he is playing into my strength – dipping passing shots. My game is structured so that I can direct the flow of play with steadiness, yet counterpunch against an aggressive net rusher. In other words, I don't need to take chances with a killer serve and risky full-bore volleys. I win without having the traditional big game – which should be music to everyone's ears, because the serve and volley are the game's two most difficult strokes to master.

In a sense, my design of play is perfect when used against those pros who learn their tennis 'by the book'. The 'book' methods are so routine that the unorthodox player has a big edge – he will always face foes who play according to predictable patterns. The traditionalists, on the other hand, can be upset by challengers committed to the unconventional and unexpected.

Rally Position

Another example of my ignoring standard instruction is my court position *during* a rally. Most 'experts' recommend that forehands and backhands should be tackled from approximately two feet behind the baseline. I double, and sometimes triple, that. Why? Because the exchange of groundstrokes is a game of attrition. If the baseline style is played properly, no one hits a winner from the backcourt.

There is no percentage in taking a wild poke at a forehand and hoping it will hit an inch from the sideline corner and scoot for a winner. The odds are stacked against this ploy. First, in aiming for such a small target on court, the chances are you'll miss it outright. Perhaps, by some miracle, the ball may land safely, but if you're up against a laser-fast runner like Gerulaitis, he'll track the shot down, anyhow, and you'll have to start all over again with double the odds loaded against you this time.

What is incredible to be about the 'experts'' advice on court positioning, is that no distinction is made between slow and fast surfaces. On clay, there is no reason not to give yourself plenty of time to run down shot after shot. Standing far behind the baseline gives you an opportunity to retrieve, with little fear that your foe can attack your defensive scurrying.

However, on a fast grass court, the ball tends to skid and stay low meaning you have to move closer to the baseline to scoop up the ball before it bounces twice. On cement or asphalt, groundstrokes move with greater velocity than on clay and that requires a position nearer the baseline, otherwise the ball will get out of range too quickly. Also there is a difference between returning a ball which has lost its power and returning a ball, from the same location, that still has plenty of force behind it.

What all this really means is that you should be flexible in your overall approach to tennis. Don't get trapped by cast iron rules. Just as every player is either taller, shorter, lighter, heavier, stronger, or weaker than his opponent, so too do situations and abilities to meet them vary enormously from player to player.

For instance, being two-handed means that my reach is shorter on the backhand than every 'one-handed' player. This suggests that I need more time to get into position anywhere on court, and that, particularly on the volley, I must prepare my approach to net more carefully than Gerulaitis or McEnroe, who both have machine-gun reactions in the forecourt.

But the best example of the need for adaptability is at Wimbledon. Since I have won Wimbledon four times in a row, it is difficult to argue that my tennis is inflexible. This great Championship is the only major title on grass – and the pros must adjust to the surface remarkably quickly to survive even a few rounds.

To the true Wimbledon expert, there must also be a subtle but crucial adjustment made between the first and second weeks at Wimbledon. During the first five days of play on the sacred surface at the All England Club, the pitch is lush, green, and fast, forcing lightning low bounces, and sometimes no bounces at all. The forceful servers tend to have unusual success the first week, even if the rest of their game is not of the same high standard. I am forced to serve and volley the first week because I can't afford to let the ball touch the ground, so erratic and rapid is its bounce.

But by the second week, the grass has become worn down and is brown from the heavy pounding of hundreds of tennis shoes on the turf. The Centre Court is so packed and solid that it plays very much like clay, my favourite surface. By the quarter-finals, the playing surface is so even and true that I can afford the luxury of staying back on serve and swapping groundstrokes. That's my strength.

If my message about the demand for innovation and originality in tennis is still not getting through, it should encourage every novice to know that the very first thing I did in tennis was wrong according to all the teaching pros. I used the western forehand grip with a closed racket face, which everyone said was too wristy and unreliable. I was told that no modern champion used the western grip and I was given a lot of advice in the beginning to change to a more accepted approach. Well, my forehand has become my best shot. I'm glad I didn't listen.

The point is that tennis is a highly personalized game. You should do what seems to work for you, rather than be regimented into a lockstep stroke that may be safe and easy to teach, but does not allow your unique talent to emerge.

My backhand is equally unorthodox, double-handed, with a closed racket face, and full of wrist. Because my basic foundation in stroke mechanics is so untraditional, the results are also unusual. For instance, the bedrock of all groundstroke instructions is to hit the ball with great depth, i.e. 'a ball hitting within a foot of the baseline is an excellent shot'. Not the way I play tennis. I believe successful tennis is a game of consistency and of taking advantage of proper percentages. Though my passing shots often look spectacular, there is a huge safety factor built into them.

Spin and Depth

If I strike a groundstroke that land a foot from my opponent's baseline, it's a mistake, because I'm only aiming for two yards past the service box, for security. My groundstrokes are so wristy that it would be impossible to control a ball aimed for the baseline with regularity. I do get depth, however, by using murderous topspin, which carries the ball deep into the backcourt after the bounce. In this fashion I achieve depth and keep a margin for error.

All this is possible because of my 'crazy' western forehand grip and my wristy two-handed backhand, both of which force me to hit with exaggerated overspin. Violent topspin is my trademark, and if I hadn't had the courage to improvise when I was young, and shatter the conventional beliefs about grips and depth, I might still be struggling through the qualifying rounds at Wimbledon, rather than aiming for a string of successive titles.

I'm advising you not to be preoccupied by rigid rules of instruction; learn your own talents and never be afraid of experimenting with what suits your game best. Remember, I'm trying to teach you to get the ball *and* your mind over the net.

7. Getting the ball over the net

I don't believe you can teach from a book, 'hit the forehand twenty centimetres in front of your left foot, and your backhand at sixty degrees'. That's nonsense. The books tell you a hundred different things and then you go out on court and try to remember all hundred rules on how to hit your forehand. Just go out and hit the stroke and see how it works. Of course there are a few adjustments you can make, but most of the good advice you get won't come in books. You must find out how it feels for you. If I were teaching a beginner, I'd make him watch me hit a few strokes and then I'd put the racket in his hand and let him try. You can never say that any one thing is right for everyone.

For example, the classic eastern forehand grip is taught as the 'shake hands grip', i.e. 'hold the racket directly in front of you with the strings perpendicular to the ground and then shake hands with the handle.' A basic problem with this suggestion is that everyone is likely to shake hands somewhat differently. Try it. Shake hands with half a dozen players at your club. One will give you a 'white knuckle' (a hard squeeze that turns your knuckles white), one will offer the 'limp fish', one the fingers closed 'hammer grip', one the 'artist's grope' (fingers extended all over your palm and wrist), one a 'tip of the fingers' grab, and maybe one the normal firm, but not death, grip, fingers slightly apart. The variety is endless, and so is the variety of grips.

My grips are anything but standard. I use the western grip for my forehand, which is rare among the pros. For the backhand, I use the more accepted eastern grip, though my application is different from the norm – I drop my wrists so the racket head is below the level of my hand. The racket for my return of serve rests in the backhand grip, and for all other strokes, forehand volley, backhand volley, serve and overhead, I use the continental grip (see photos).

It's very important to hit the ball well in front of your hips. You can't see the ball properly when it gets past your body. None of the pros hits the ball behind them. Gerulaitis is occasionally late on his forehand, and so is Panatta, but he's so talented he can hit the ball with his hands over his eyes. Yet on the volley, don't hit as far in front of you as the books say. Hold your racket way in front of you and see how flimsy it is. A ball hitting it in this position would receive no power. Now put your racket just slightly in front of you with your elbow pushed into your side and feel the power and leverage.

Before 1976, when I came to net, I used the same grip as for my groundstrokes which meant the forehand volley was hit with a western grip. It was impossible. That's why I had so many problems with my volley. If someone hit a dink to my forehand or backhand I usually dumped it into the net. When I changed to the continental grip I felt I had more time and I could hit low balls effectively. I made the change myself. I tried it more and more in practice. I saw everyone else use the continental, and I decided that if I was going to learn to volley, I'd better switch. No one had to tell me.

Other than this case of volley, I never learned by imitation. I know others do, and it's an excellent teaching aid, watching the stars play, but I rarely notice the player. I follow the point instead. It never worried me that everyone else was using different grips and strokes. I was stubborn.

Rod Laver was my childhood idol but the first time I saw him in person was the 1971 Wimbledon when he lost to Tom Gorman. Before that I watched him on TV, but his only influence on me was how he behaved on court, not his strokes. I admired his concentration and straight face. He never got upset. I wasn't too surprised on those rare occasions when he lost because he was playing with a Chemold metal racket and I remember everyone in the locker room said the racket was no good.

Backhand

There are many schools of thought about the advantages and disadvantages of the two-handed backhand. For example, some say that two hands share the work so it's less tiring; others say that because both hands are involved it's more tiring. I do know that I have to prepare for the stroke earlier, and bend my knees more on the two-handed shot than on my one-handed forehand. Other than that, I can only say that it works for me.

I place my right hand on the racket as if the stroke were a standard one-handed eastern backhand. The left hand is placed above the right

Backhand grip

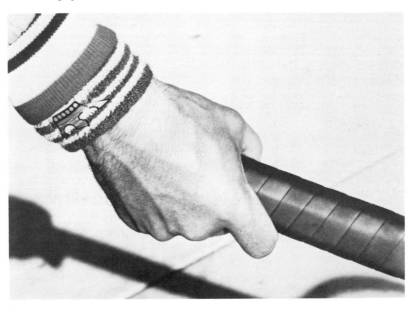

Forehand grip

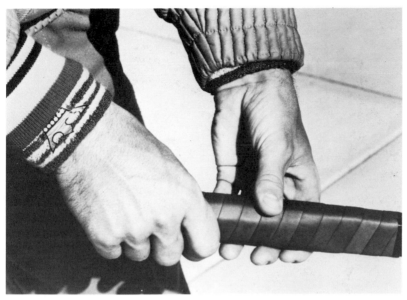

Return on serve grip

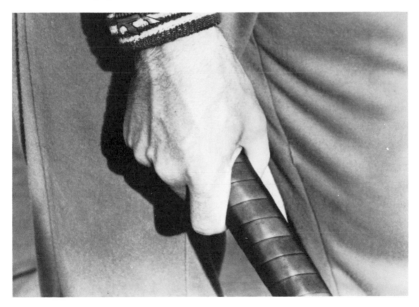

Continental grip (used for forehand and backhand volley, serve, and overhead)
(*Credit: E.L. Scott*)

I meet a high backhand well in front of my right hip (left) (*Credit: Art Seitz*)

Early racket preparation is particularly important on the backhand (right) (*Credit: Art Seitz*)

Here's the beginning of my forward swing on the backhand. Note that the racket face is below the level of my wrists (left) (*Credit: Kathy Finnerty*)

My backhand follow through (right) (*Credit: Kathy Finnerty*)

in such a position that I could hit a choked up left-handed western forehand if I took my right hand away. I bring the racket back slightly below my knees and close to my side with a small loop on the way back and both wrists cocked downwards. I actually drop the racket face below the level of my wrists to exaggerate the racket head sweep from low to high which also exaggerates the amount of topspin put on the return.

Jimmy Connors, on the other hand, brings his racket straight back with a firm, straight wrist slightly below his waist. Our different style results in a different type of shot. Connors's is flat, hard, and deep, clearing the net by a few inches; but mine relies heavily on overspin, clearing the net by a foot or more and with varying depths.

As I pull the racket forward, my wrists explode the racket face under the ball snapping upwards to shoot tremendous topspin into the shot. My right shoulder which had turned so that it pointed towards the net on the backswing is parallel to the net at the end of the stroke with the racket head finishing to my right, two feet above my head on the follow through. But the follow through changes a lot on every stroke depending on where the ball has bounced, where I want to hit it, and how much time I have.

My backhand is built for my game of patience in the backcourt and topspin passing shots, while Connors's backhand is an offensive weapon, hit aggressively to draw a short return so he can attack at net. If I had to compare Connors's and my backhand in a single phrase, mine is efficient, his flamboyant.

Forehand

My grip on the forehand is western, with the heel of the racket inside my palm, enabling my wrists to whip the racket faster as it catches the ball. My stance is often open which gives me more time to hit and get back into position. I use my left hand to help take my racket back. My backswing has a high loop, and I meet the ball well in front of my left hip (right hip in the open stance) striking between four and five o'clock, if you imagine the ball as the face of a clock. I snap my wrists upward in a sweeping motion, rolling the racket face over at the end of contact and carrying the racket over my left shoulder on the follow through – often so it is pointing directly behind me.

Despite the speed of my arm and racket as they strike the ball, my feet stay firmly on the ground and my hips move only slightly, not rolling forward the way a golfer's do. Keeping the lower body stable and low reduces power somewhat, but it is the key to my consistency.

The secret of my forehand is dropping the racket head below the ball so the upward swing can produce wild topspin. Topspin can also be generated from the eastern grip but not to the same extent. I sacrifice depth with my heavy emphasis on spin, but I think consistency is more important – not hitting over the baseline or into the net.

Serve

'Newcombe's or Gonzalez's serve was like an axe – Borg's is like a rigger's knife, sharp and practical.'
Tennis Week, February 1980

I don't serve as hard as Tanner, Nastase, Pat DuPre, Peter Fleming, or McEnroe, but my first serve is effective because it is difficult to pick. My motion is simple, with no fancy wind-up, and I hit it down the line or at an angle from the same toss, making its direction difficult to anticipate. My second serve has pretty heavy spin and, while it's not an offensive weapon, no one can attack it easily.

I keep the second ball in my left pocket, not my hand, because I need my left hand for the two fisted backhand, but I also think it's a good idea anyway. Fetching the ball from the pocket makes you slow down instead of rushing the second serve after the first fault. In addition, a free left hand is a better guide when taking the racket back on both forehand and backhand strokes.

My service motion is very simple, though I have had problems with my toss in the past. You want to make sure the toss goes straight up and does not move in an arc. I face the side of the court when I start to serve and if my toss is straight in front of me the ball has a tendency to sail slightly backwards over my head in a curve. To offset this problem, I toss the ball in front of my left side towards the net.

In 1976, when Lennart and I decided I had to improve my serve, the first thing we did was change my foot positioning at the start of the serve. My right or trailing foot is now directly behind my front foot, which forms the top of the letter T. With my trailing foot this far behind, I feel more of my body gets into the serve, not just my arm as before. John McEnroe exaggerates this trailing foot position even more with his back foot almost touching the baseline. My follow through is conventional with the racket ending up past my left side.

The middle of the loop on my forehand backswing (left)   (*Credit: Art Seitz*)

Just before contact on a low bounce to my forehand. The racket face is well below wrist level and the shot requires keen concentration (right)
(*Credit: Kathy Finnerty*)

My forehand follow through (opposite)   (*Credit: Kathy Finnerty*)

On my serve you can see that the grip is well within the palm of my right hand. Also, I'm standing sideways to the net, almost until contact with the ball (*Credit: Art Seitz*)

My follow through on the serve (opposite)   (*Credit: Art Seitz*)

Tennis doesn't often reward the dazzling shot, especially on a slow surface. For instance, if you hit a marvellous flat serve deep into the backhand corner on clay, it is a bootless tactic. The speed and depth are blunted by the court, and the risk, energy, and concentration required to deliver such a well-placed and powerful serve is simply not worth it.

I do put an enormous amount of spin on both my first and second serves for consistency, and the second is not aimed anywhere close to the lines. I just put it deep in the middle of the service box with enough spin to stop my opponent chipping and charging the net. I never try to win the point outright on my serve – nor should you. In the finals of the French Championships in 1979 I didn't serve a single ace. The most I do is change direction and the amount of spin, for surprise. I may make Connors miss my serve because he is caught off-guard but not because I ace him.

On a fast surface – grass, cement, or a slick indoor supreme court – it is smart for a good server to go for the ace. The percentages are now better because if the ball goes in hard, the surface won't slow it down. In other words, you get a reward for a lightning serve at Wimbledon, while at the French it usually doesn't help at all.

The problem about beginners and intermediates going for a bullet first serve is that if they miss they're faced with having to get the second one in. This is the most embarrassing situation for any player – the humiliation of hitting a double fault. Avoid it by concentrating totally on hitting the second serve. Don't bother practising the first. Anyone can hit the ball hard, but only a handful in the world can put the hard ones in with any consistency. The old theory that 'you are only as good as your second serve' is one of the few lessons from the past that is still true – even for the superstars. After I broke Tanner's serve in the first game of the fifth set in the 1979 Wimbledon finals, my first serves were nothing but good second serves for the rest of the day. In other words, I played it safe because I didn't want Tanner to see a first serve miss and thus gain confidence knowing a second serve was coming. That way he'd be attacking the net on my service games. Roscoe obviously is from another school. He banged over two dozen unplayable serves against me in five sets. But I won the match.

Perhaps the best example for ninety-eight per cent of the world's players is that of Chris Evert Lloyd playing Tracy Austin in the 1979 US Open final, on a fast asphalt surface, when neither hit an ace in the match but they played each other beautifully and wisely. The ace is a dramatic shot – like the home run in baseball – but it may destroy your sense of tactics by tempting you to hit the ball harder than is safe. A simple home run can win a baseball game but a single ace can't win a tennis match.

One of the temptations intermediate players have is to follow their serves to net just like the 'big boys'. Even at my level of the game I think this is wrong. But at lower levels I think the strategy is invariably suicidal. It may work sometimes, but you'll probably remember your one brilliant cross-court volley and forget about your two flubs and the passing shot. The volley is the toughest shot to master, and if you serve and just hit a safe volley, it is a set-up for your foe's forehand. In other words, his groundstrokes are better than your volley, and unless you prepare your way carefully to volley by rallying until you get a short ball, and then underspinning a deep approach, you'll find yourself at net begging to be passed.

Volley

One of the main reasons the volley is the most difficult stroke to perfect is that no one practises the volley one tenth as much as any other stroke. When we start to rally most of us hit for ten minutes in the backcourt, come to net for five volleys, two overheads, and then say, 'I'm ready, let's play.'

The problem about learning the volley properly is that it can't be practised politely. What we all do is go to net and hit the volley right back to our practice partner so he won't get annoyed by our 'rude' put-aways. The bad habit starts here. The volley is supposed to be an offensive weapon. There should be no such thing as a steady volleyer. You're not at the net to rally. But when you practise one up, one back, you never get a sense of putting the volley away. The only way this can be learned is by using a ball machine whose feelings can't be hurt when you go for volley winners, or by getting a third practice mate and rotating the one person at net with two in the backcourt so that everyone gets a chance at hitting the volley aggressively. With two players at the baseline, the balls that would have been 'rude' put-aways with one person will be returned. If a third player isn't available, at least station the baseline person in the backhand or forehand side of the court to give a semblance of reality to the practice session. Few players hit their volley down the middle and live to talk about it.

I credit the best teaching line about volleying to Pancho Gonzalez, who said that when he was at net he hit the ball pretending the barrier was not there. 'I don't volley over the net', Pancho explained, 'I volley into the court.' Pancho's advice may be the first Zen tennis advice. It makes sense. How many of us worry about getting the ball over the net when we should be worrying about aiming for a space in the backcourt?

On the backhand volley, I get my racket back shoulder high past my left ear with the racket pointing behind my body. I only have half as big a wind-up on my forehand volley. When you don't have much time you can only block or punch at the volley, but if you have hit a good approach shot, you should be prepared to take a solid crack at the ball. The volley is supposed to be an offensive stroke, and if you're not prepared to put the ball away, you shouldn't be at net. How often do you see a net man hit a defensive safe volley and get passed by the next shot? I come to net as often in a match as I do in practice – which on a slow surface (clay, Har-Tru, Fast-Dri) is five per cent of the time. On a faster surface the percentage may increase to ten per cent but no more.

I don't bend my knees as low as Connors. His bending must take a lot of energy out of him. Connors bends so much and gets so low to the ball that his right knee sometimes touches the court surface. A statistics expert once estimated that in a normal two-set match on clay lasting one hour, there are approximately 2,500 ball hits, not including faults. If I bent my knees as low as Connors I'd be exhausted, considering 1,250 of those ball hits were mine. Part-time players aren't in the same shape that Connors is in, and I'd advise you not to copy him. You don't have to bend your knees so much to play properly. But we both meet the ball well in front of our hips and, like all two-handers, must prepare the stroke extra early.

Gene Scott: If one looks for the origins of Bjorn's game, which combine the apparent contradiction of thunderous topspin and metronome steadiness, we find there is no contradiction at all. The topspin is, after all, the means to his consistency. If his style looks like ping-pong without rushing the net, it is no accident. His father, Rune, narrowly missed being included in the Swedish table-tennis team twice, and the influence of ping-pong is everywhere in Borg's strokes. One of Bjorn's childhood games was makeshift ping-pong, using books as a net on the dining-room table.

Tennis demanded that he learn a counter-attack

stroke which ping-pong did not require – the passing shot. Borg could have chosen the flashy flat pass or the conservative slice of many of his Swedish forebears, Jan Erik Lindquist, Sven Davidson, or his own coach, Lennart Bergelin. Characteristically, he selected instead a method that was safer than no-spin and more effective than underspin. Excessive topspin would clear the net by a foot or more yet dip at the attacker's feet. It has force, deception, and consistency. It is also in the immediate family of his groundstrokes. He does not have to adjust his motion from groundstroke to passing shot. Many players have an arsenal of shots so varied that the sheer weight of choice is confusing and obstructs what should be an easy flow in the game.

Beginners and Topspin

Obviously a beginner has trouble making contact with the ball so my topspin trademark is not appropriate until you have a proper sense of timing and reasonably strong wrists.

A beginner has to concentrate on the basics which include taking the racket straight back with no loops or fancy hitches and rotating the shoulders simultaneously. The wrist should be slightly cocked with the racket head just above the level of the wrists. The arc of the swing should be from a little below the hip to head height. The beginner should keep a firm wrist throughout the forehand and backhand stroke. Ideally, the left foot should be parallel to the net and two feet in front of the right foot on the forehand, and on the backhand the right foot should be parallel to the net and two feet in front of the left foot. But tennis is not played under ideal conditions. You never get a ball dropped carefully a foot in front of your body so you can deliberate slowly on your stroke. You are hitting a moving ball while moving yourself. A beginner is rarely successful at staying low to the ball and following it through. More often he retreats awkwardly and makes his hit with left or right leg raised off the ground. He is perilously close to falling over. A sense of balance and timing cannot be taught by a book. It must be learned on court by constantly experiencing the speed and spin of balls coming from every direction.

There are two basic schools of thought on how to develop terrific topspin. One is to start swinging the racket slowly with slight overspin and, once your confidence and timing are developed, to pick up the velocity of the stroke gradually, until the wrist snap and swing are going at full speed. The other technique is to start immediately with full topspin, which means hitting a lot of balls into the net and over the fence, but the theory is that once you've mastered the speed, there is no further adjustment required. I feel that is the right technique. The graduated method is not efficient because as you learn each step it must be unlearned when you pick up more pace.

So that you don't lose practice partners as often as you lose balls in the car park, my advice is to practise your topspin with a ball machine hitting hundreds of balls at full speed until you get the feel of the wrist snap and are catching the ball just right. Your first target should just be the centre of the court and, as you develop your timing, you should alter your aim gradually, from side to side.

I know two of the past greats, Don Budge and Jack Kramer, have kidded about my topspin shots, which sometimes land shallow near the service line. One of Budge's favourite quips is that he hit his serve with greater depth than my groundstrokes. To respond to this would get me into the same sort of never ending argument as who was better, Bill Tilden or Rod Laver? I guess I don't care what the old timers think. The last Hall of Famer I listened to told me I could never win Wimbledon with a western forehand, a two-handed backhand and not coming to net. I'm willing to let my record speak for itself.

8. Getting your mind over the net

'Borg has tunnel vision. He pays the price. He can stay on court literally all day hitting forehands and backhands. He wants to be out there in 100°, in the humidity, under a boiling sun.'
Billie Jean King

Tennis racket design didn't change for almost a hundred years. The construction was wooden and egg-shaped for a century. It makes you wonder what sort of people made rackets – were they made of wood and egg-shaped too? Tennis instruction has suffered from the same lack of innovation for almost as long. Players have been fed an identical patter for years, as if all abilities were equal and as if what made sense for one athlete made sense for another, with no sense of the individual taken into account.

To learn the full range of any stroke, and for adjustments to be made as the learning process goes on, variety should not only be permitted, but is essential. For instance, if you put too much wrist into any shot, one correction is to move the hand further up the handle so the butt end comes out of the palm and prevents a floppy wrist. My standard grip on both forehand and backhand has the butt end of the racket flush against the fleshy part of my right palm, which means that my hand overlaps the end of the racket. This makes my wrist flexible so that it can snap violently at the ball giving enormous topspin. However, if I suggested the same grip to a student trying to learn flat deep groundstrokes, it would be disastrous. For precision and accuracy on forehands and backhands with no spin, a firm wrist is essential. Grasping the handle so that the heel sticks slightly out of the hand is one way to accomplish a stiff wrist.

Spin

Grips and spin are closely related and both involve making a choice when you are deciding what sort of game you want to play. The more spin you put on the ball the more power you lose. Jimmy Connors hits the ball harder than I do, but his passing shots are sometimes not as effective as mine because they have little deception and no margin for error. When Jimmy is on good form he is devastating because even if you know where he is going to hit the ball, he hits so hard that anticipation doesn't help. But, day by day, my results may be better because my passes are more consistent, and it is difficult to volley my ball dipping at your feet. Connors's drives rise as they go over the net and a good volleyer prefers this to hitting below the net.

There is one concept that you should understand before you decide which style you prefer – topspin with reduced power but a good safety margin, or flat with more power but less safety margin. My topspin is safe not because it is accurate in depth. On a passing shot I don't care whether the ball lands close to the baseline or the service line. If the ball passes the man at net, it doesn't count more if it lands on the baseline. But I do need a ball that goes straight and is not affected by the wind. Topspin, no matter how wristy, can go straight as a string down the line, or cross-court, and will not be blown off line by a gust of wind as easily as will a flat or sliced ball.

The second reason topspin is safe is because it clears the net by a larger margin than a flat or sliced shot. It is not important whether the ball clears the net by six inches or two feet on sinking shots. The difference to your opponent between your clearing the net by six inches or two feet is his choice of hitting the volley off the top of his shoe or below his knees – both are difficult. A hard flat ground stroke on the other hand has to skim the net closely to be effective, increasing the chances for the ball to hit the net. And a slice, while it can clear the net by a wide margin in baseline rallies, is useless as a passing shot unless one has the genius for precision that Ken Rosewall had.

The one drawback of topspin for beginners and intermediate players is that you must have remarkable timing to avoid hitting the ball off the frame. If you're having difficulty making proper contact, go back to hitting flat, keeping the stroke as simple as possible. Remember the style you decide on should be dictated by your own ability and not by a desire to copy Connors or me.

For me, topspin is preferable for many reasons. Not only does it disturb net rushers, but it allows for my steadiness in the backcourt. I can clear the net with enormous safety, and even if the ball lands short at the service line, the spin will carry the ball past the baseline. So I have the best of both worlds – safety plus depth. Naturally, against a good player, I hit at an opponent's service line at my peril. He is very

Part of 'getting your mind over the net' is the feeling that you are a champion (opposite) (*Credit: E.L. Scott*)

likely to pounce on the ball and come to net. But he has to hit a perfect approach or my topspin pass will be at his feet. I try to keep my groundstrokes between the service line and baseline and let the topspsin provide the rest of the stroke's depth, but I do have the safety valve of knowing that, although a slight mishit may change the depth by two or three feet, the ball will still land in court. A hard flat hitter like Connors doesn't have that luxury, since he is aiming for the vicinity of the baseline every time. If he hits slightly off centre, his two or three foot variation will lose him the point.

There are two other reasons why I prefer the topspin approach. One is that not only is the dipping action treacherous for a volleyer, but the shot is very flexible. You can change its direction at the last minute by flipping the wrist, making the shot impossible to read. And finally the topspin arc of the ball gives you more time to recover from an off-court position. The result is that topspin combines a safe yet deceptive offensive weapon with defensive features built in.

Teaching

Kids eight-years old don't respond to the words, 'take your racket back', 'watch the ball', and 'bend your knees', as well as they do to their own instincts of how to hit the ball. Saying, 'watch the ball' is insulting to a child. Of course he's trying to watch the ball. Saying too much is distracting. 'Take your racket back' is another standard phrase. It's silly. Of course he'll take the racket back without being told to. What is useful is to urge the youngster to take his racket back early because that advice helps straight away. He'll have more time to prepare the stroke. You can even elaborate on this point by advising him to take his racket back when the ball passes over the net. This gives him a target to think about. Saying, 'bend your knees' is meaningless. No youngster with any athletic ability will hit even his first shot stiff-legged. He'll do what's comfortable. John McEnroe and Peter Fleming stand almost straight up when they hit the ball while Jimmy Connors goes almost to his knees on every forehand and backhand. But that takes a lot of energy. Generally I'd recommend having a stance that is a compromise between proper balance and comfort.

A golfer addresses the ball with his hips at right angles to the direction of the shot, and, at the moment of impact, his hips rotate rapidly so that on follow-through they face straight down the fairway.

There is little such hip rotation in tennis. My hips remain perfectly still at impact and, even on follow-through, rarely move in the direction of the ball. Also, I never lift off my feet on follow-through, no matter how hard I swing at the ball. Many players jump off the ground when they hit topspin because the violent upward motion of the stroke takes them off their feet. I maintain that for both power and accuracy the momentum of the swing should not be *up* but forward. There is very little movement in my lower body when I swing. My wrist, arm, and shoulder provide all the power I need. If the rest of my body gets involved in the stroke there is too much unnecessary motion which destroys the stroke's precision.

In choosing basic styles – groundstrokes or volleys or a combination of both – you should be aware that, even for a weekend player, staying in the backcourt will take more out of you than volleying. You will have to be in better shape to rally all day than to end points quickly by moving to net. With each opponent you must weigh the factors: am I in better condition? Am I steadier? Do I have a better volley?

Try to make the choice simple. Reduce the game to its simplest terms so you don't have to worry about execution of shots you don't have. Most players learn how to hit groundstrokes first. The volley is the game's most difficult stroke to learn, not only because its mechanics are intricate, but because the time spent learning the volley is so proportionately small.

What is anticipation? It is moving to the right part of the court before your opponent hits the ball. Part of this is simply experience, knowing the best shot for the other man to hit in every situation. For example, if you are both in the backcourt and you hit a backhand deep to your opponent's backhand, the safest shot is for him to return to your backhand. So you'd move instinctively in this direction. Yet if you came to net behind the same deep approach to the backhand, you'd lean to the forehand forecourt because the court angle makes it impossible for him to play the same safe cross-court shot without your cutting it off at the net.

What are the most important points in a match? For once, convention is correct on the subject; 15-30, 30-15, break point, and the first point of every game. But I've never hesitated by considering how I was going to win these points. I have played so many practice matches and so many tournaments that my game is instinctive. When I'm even, or ahead, and have a long point to play – break point, set point or ad against me – my instinct is always to play safe. If I'm behind, I take a

The problem with standardized instruction is that it confuses students who see the pros do things differently from what their instructors advise. The fact is that I almost never hit the ball exactly the same way twice. My backhand and forehand follow throughs, shown above and opposite, are not typical even for me, but each worked on these particular shots   (*Credit: E.L. Scott*)

chance and go for it. If I'm going to lose I don't care.

I don't have four different ways to play, I just have one game – topspin, and patience from the backcourt. Because the plan is simple, it is easier to concentrate, there are no distractions, no problems.

I don't have to rely on a particular strategy other than keeping the ball deep and high over the net to cut down on errors – nor do I use any rally sequence if an opponent has a weakness. Selecting shots to probe his weaknesses is done at random. In this way I can play by instinct and not get bogged down by having to think where I'm going to place the ball each time.

The process of deliberating how and where to hit the ball is incredibly tiring, and because I have the ability to turn on the 'automatic pilot' and not fret over each shot is one reason why spectators think I'm 'so cool under pressure'. Doctors say my low pulse rate is healthy too, because it means my heart is so efficient. It has to pump fewer times a minute to send the blood through my system than an opponent's heart may have to, to accomplish the same function.

Training

One of the worst ways tennis players abuse themselves is in what they drink at the courtside. Usually it is whatever product is supplied free to the tournament director in exchange for the beverage company's exposures on court; Coca Cola, iced tea, Tab, Pepsi, etc. Often these companies pay enormous fees to have exclusive identification at courtside – Coca Cola pays the US Open $250,000 per year to have their giant coke sign above the scoreboard and their coolers by the umpire's chair. Other smaller events receive $2,500 to $25,000 each, depending on television coverage. When a company pays this sort of money, they insist on having their product on hand in their cooler and served in their cups. The tournament director does nothing to refuse this, although a player is perfectly within his rights to bring his own drink to the court. Some do. But ninety per cent of the touring pros simply drink what the sponsor has put in the cooler.

Jimmy Connors, for example, drinks Coca Cola throughout his match. I drink water only. During a three-hour practice session, I will drink three quarts of cold water – reducing the amount during a three hour match to a quart. Neither Lennart nor I subscribe to the theory that cold liquids give you stomach cramps. We feel that if you're hot, cold water cools you off, warm water does not. In any case, I've been drinking iced water for the sixteen years of my tennis career and never have had stomach cramps.

My training for a tournament is done before it starts. Once a tournament begins, I rarely practise for more than an hour unless I have a day off. My warm-up before a final is even less, twenty minutes to a half an hour, just as a guitarist picks and tunes before a concert. This session really isn't for practice at all but for timing. If I had a vigorous session right before an important match, it would take the edge off my playing. If I'm not in shape by Sunday, I won't improve by hitting for two hours that morning.

I never run for conditioning before or during any championship. The only time I've ever jogged is when I'm at home for a rest. I gain weight very easily without tennis so I go out then for a run to keep my weight around 160 lbs.

I think for others it is a good idea to run – not long distances like the marathon runners or even the joggers – but short-step running. Quick sprints are helpful. You don't run a mile in a tennis match, you run a thousand ten-foot races. I do all my running on court by practising four, five and six hours a day.

I don't stay away from any foods in particular. I eat bread, butter, milk and ice cream which are all traditionally too fatty for an athlete's diet, but I don't care what I eat when I'm playing. I burn up all the foods I eat so I never gain weight. Obviously, if you only play at weekends it's hard to rid your system of junk foods. If we have a giant steak and potatoes on the same night, and the next day I play five sets of tennis and you don't, you'll wear your meal around your middle for a month. And every extra pound you carry around is a huge handicap. Just imagine putting a five pound weight in your shorts and trying to play tennis.

When I stop playing I do watch what I eat, avoiding sweets and often only taking one meal a day. I don't like spirits and only drink wine and beer. I've never smoked.

I know my diet of meat and vegetables is old fashioned for athletes. The accepted training meal today is a menu loaded with carbohydrates like bread, potatoes and all forms of pasta. Tennis players first heard of this when Adriano Panatta was seen preparing for the French and Italian Opens on large helpings of spaghetti. The players scoffed at him at first saying this was another example of the talented Italian's lack of discipline. Then he won both the Italian and the French Opens in 1976, and people listened.

Lob

One more myth is how difficult the topspin lob is. This is nonsense. The reason it seems so impossible is that no one practises it. Have you ever seen a player with a basket of balls go on to a court and practise his topspin lob? Of course not. The same is true of the drop shot. No one works on craft and disguise in practice (at least you try the drop shot in enough matches over the years to develop a feel for the stroke). But because it's considered rude to your partner to practise something he can't work on at the same time, both the topspin lob and drop shot are neglected. The answer, of course, is to talk to your practice partner about the problem and to take turns developing these unpractised strokes. The topspin lob, because of its deception, adds incredible dimensions to your game and is possibly easier to hit than a good deep flat lob. (Anyone can hit a ball up in the air and call it a lob, but the accuracy and timing required to lift a ball with no spin while on the run close to the baseline is extremely delicate.) And, in fact, the topspin lob doesn't have to be as deep as the flat one because it's so difficult to read.

I do not lob well defensively because, having so much confidence in my passing shots, I don't practise the defensive lob. I like the offensive lob which is a sudden high topspinner hit from the same stance as a passing shot – so the net man is leaning forward when the ball sails over his head.

Percentage Tennis

My conservative game forces rivals to take chances. If they do, the percentages work for me during the whole match. If an opponent like Roscoe Tanner serves twenty-five aces against me in a match he'll probably win, but he can't do this very often. My game forces him to play low percentage tennis.

Percentage tennis means different things to different players. Jack Kramer's percentage tennis represents the traditional thinking which used to make sense. 'Never serve to your opponent's forehand on a big point' and 'always underspin your approach (so it stays low forcing him to hit up) to your opponent's backhand' were Kramer mainstays. And for his era, they worked. In the old days no one, except Don Budge, had a backhand weapon – one that was more dangerous than the forehand. Today, there are a dozen players including Arthur Ashe,

Jimmy Connors, Cliff Drysdale, John McEnroe, and myself, who like nothing better than a foe who hits to our backhand on a big point.

My definition of percentage tennis is different. It's not so much a matter of whether I hit to my opponent's forehand or backhand, because I think I can run down any attack and counterpunch effectively no matter where the ball is hit. My synonym for percentage tennis is *patience*. I want to hit one more ball in court than my rival hits. I want him to think I'm much more patient so he'll make a mistake either in execution (racket error) or in picking a low percentage ripper for the lines. This philosophy works for beginners too. If a novice (or intermediate for that matter) plays my way, he will aim most of his shots cross-court where there is more room for mistakes. If you aim a ball down the line and miss by an inch, you'll lose the point. Yet if you always think cross-court you can miss by two yards or more and still have the ball land safely in court.

Even I practise these beginner's patterns when having difficulty adjusting to strange conditions or to a particular opponent. I keep the ball in the centre of the court waiting until I have control of my strokes.

Kramer was the first proponent of the Big Game in which he followed both his first serve and second serve to net on any fast surface and rushed in to volley even on his opponent's serve. Jack's percentages were set forth in terms of all-out attack. Frankly, this appears to be a contradiction to me. I'm not saying he wasn't successful. He was. And he certainly was a great player. But he didn't play percentage tennis the way I think of it – in terms of safety and caution. A net rusher is not playing it safe. He is daring you to pass him. Kramer won because he was bold and had the skills to back it up. He didn't play percentage tennis.

My 'percentages' have more to do with my mind than my strokes. I try to make my challenger believe he can't outsteady me. My cold attitude on court helps. I never applaud or acknowledge an opponent's good shot. I just go about the business of the next point. This, in a sense, is saying, 'I don't care how spectacular one shot is, you'll have to hit two thousand exactly like it to beat me.'

Remember that at the top levels of the game, weaknesses and strengths are only relative. In a sense, there are no weaknesses but only comparative strengths. But this is not entirely true. There are fifty players who can volley better than Vilas or I can, but we have both found that if our groundstrokes are good enough, we literally don't need a volley to win. We can't be as reluctant to come up to net as

Harold Solomon, but we both understand that we volley for surprise and to add a sudden dimension to our games when our opponents least expect it.

Gene Scott: There is a standard litany offered by instructors when Borg's name is brought up. 'No one else can play the way he does', or 'I'd never try to teach Bjorn Borg's strokes'. Because the Swede's strokes are unorthodox and he was, to a large extent, self-taught, tennis teachers cringe at the prospect of their students imitating Borg's style. That is a commentary about the reactionary mentality of teaching pros more than anything else. The fact that Borg has won four French Opens (considered by experts as the world's clay court championships and the game's most gruelling test), and four Wimbledons in a row should mean that he must be doing something right and that there is something for the rest of the tennis world to learn from him.

Caricature by David Levine

9. My record album

In picking my ten best matches, the criteria for selection include the significance of when, and where, the match was played. For instance I didn't include the 1978 Final of the $200,000 Suntory Cup in Tokyo where I destroyed Connors, losing only four games. The event was only a four-man round-robin with enormous guarantees paid to all of us regardless of who won. It didn't have any sense of tradition and history and had no rank as an important title on the calendar. In fact, because the field was limited to four, the results counted neither for world ranking nor for official prize money. But the tennis was terrific. Even Jimmy played well. It's just that on that day I was lucky and won every big important point.

Also I don't include any losses even though I may have played well. If I had to list a few defeats I remember well, my four-setter to John Newcombe in the 1975 WCT Finals and the five-set marathon to Roger Taylor in the 1973 Wimbledon quarter-finals, come to mind. But no match I have lost helped my goal to win more major titles than any tennis player in history.

I have chosen a single match from the list to record the multiple elements of competition, with reflections on it that are something between a sketchbook and a diary.

Borg's Ten Biggest Wins

1. Davis Cup 1972	Borg d. Onny Parun	4-6, 3-6, 6-3, 6-4, 6-4
2. French Open Finals 1974	Borg d. Manuel Orantes	2-6, 6-7, 6-0, 6-1, 6-1
3. WCT Semi-final 1975	Borg d. Rod Laver	7-6, 3-6, 7-6, 6-2
4. Wimbledon Final 1976	Borg d. Ilie Nastase	6-4, 6-2, 9-7
5. Wimbledon Semi-final 1977	Borg d. Vitas Gerulaitis	6-4, 3-6, 6-3, 3-6, 8-6
6. Wimbledon Final 1977	Borg d. Jimmy Connors	3-6, 6-2, 6-1, 5-7, 6-4
7. Barcelona Grand Prix 1977	Borg d. Eddie Dibbs	6-0, 6-0, 6-2
8. Wimbledon Final 1978	Borg d. Jimmy Connors	6-2, 6-2, 6-3
9. Wimbledon Semi-final 1979	Borg d. Jimmy Connors	6-2, 6-3, 6-2
10. Masters Round Robin 1980	Borg d. Jimmy Connors	3-6, 6-3, 7-6

A few moments at Wimbledon in the course of my victories there (opposite and following pages) (*Credit: Art Seitz*)

The Match

Jimmy Connors has been my most intense rival for six years. At the moment, John McEnroe has the game to give both Jimmy and me sleepless nights. His style is flexible while Jimmy's is rigid. John can open up the entire court with his serve, and his volley is lightning, but the fury of a McEnroe/Borg rivalry has not yet had a chance to boil over. It's still simmering.

Connors and I, on the other hand, have been at each other's throats for five US Opens and four Wimbledons. I have the edge now, with fourteen to ten in total matches, but in the early days Jimmy totally intimidated me even on my favourite surface – clay.

1979 was my best year for dominating Connors, when I won six times and never lost, as well as another match at the Grand Prix Masters in 1980, which is really considered part of the 1979 season. The latter was the most exciting encounter I have ever experienced with Jimmy – maybe with anybody. Other titles have been more prestigious, or worth more in prize money, or both, but none has matched the fire of that Thursday, 10 January night at Madison Square Garden.

To set the stage, Connors was coming off a mediocre year for him – he reached the semi-finals of the French, Wimbledon, and the US Open, won the US Clay Courts and six other tournaments, and $701,340 in prize money. Mediocre for Jimmy meant that for the first time in five years he was ranked two on the computer. He had reasons for his apparent let-down. He had married former playmate of the year Patti Maguire at the end of 1978. They had a baby boy, Brett, in July of 1979 and the experience distracted Jimmy from his tennis. I could see that. He plays with such intensity and his margin for error is so low that any lapse in concentration is fatal to his game.

He kept saying that once his marriage and son were in order, he would be back. The first sign of this spirit was at the $300,000 Montreal Challenge Cup in December 1979. We both reached the finals and, although I won in four sets, the second set, which he won, was the best he had played against me in two years.

The Masters came exactly a month later and Jimmy was especially lean – he had lost almost ten pounds – and you could see electricity in his eyes. He seemed to be in a barely controlled rage all week, and it was obvious in his play.

The shame was that the round-robin pairings had Jimmy and me in the same group. After all, we were ranked number one and two in the world and should have been split up. However, the policy of the Masters is to seed players according to their standings in the Grand Prix, which rewards the number of events played and helps to encourage participation in tournaments around the world but it is poor as a method for picking seeds. As a result I would have to beat Roscoe Tanner, who had upset me at the US Open four months earlier, and Connors to reach the semi-finals.

Before I went on court that night Bill Norris, one of the official tour trainers, limbered up my legs for ten minutes with a cream from a large white bottle of Dermassage body lotion. Norris had dubbed himself 'The Wizard of Gauze', a label that he has had printed on the back of his Adidas track suit, which he parades on court at every opportunity.

The match starts at 8 p.m. Although I break Connors right away to lead 2-0 in the first set, there are sparks shooting out of his socks. Jimmy breaks back immediately and with a series of deep hard baseline exchanges, he dictates the pace of each game. This is a dedicated confident Connors I haven't seen for a long time. By 9.05 Jimmy has won the first set 6-3.

I'm playing terribly. I'm just out of the match. If I continue to play like this I won't deserve to win. Connors is on top of every ball – hitting it really well.

Connors plays a loose service game to open the second set and I break straightaway. Maybe I can get into the match. I've just got to be more aggressive. I must take some chances and attack his serve.

Lennart, sitting in the third row of Madison Square Garden's courtside seats, has not said a word. His arms are folded, and will remain so throughout the entire match, except that every so often he slowly unfolds his arms and drys his palms on the thighs of his grey flannel trousers. The only sound from Lennart is a dry crackling noise when his mouth opens, which is a sure sign of his nervousness.

My fiancée, Mariana, is sitting next to him and they will not exchange a single sentence the entire match. She sighs and bites her lips alternately, and whispers 'Jesus Christ' under her breath after every important point. It is fitting that the two people closest to me behave on the sidelines as I do on court. Quietly and intently.

Finally Lennart speaks – to no one in particular – eyes straight ahead, 'Bjorn must actually win a game – not just let Connors lose it – before he'll believe he can win.'

9.30 I miss another forehand and, if you look closely, you will see my first sign of emotion – a slight shake of my head. *9.40* I uncork a bolo forehand for a quick winner from the backcourt. *9.45* As I sit down on the changeover, I notice Andy Warhol sitting in the front row with his arms folded exactly like Lennart. *9.47* Crowd applauds a Connors fault, and I'm puzzled – if the fans behave like animals how can anyone wonder why the players don't control themselves?

There is a unique anti-clapping policy among professionals. If you look at the players' section in any stadium, it might seem curious that the pros don't applaud good shots. The reason? Showing favouritism would haunt a player who one day might face the man he cheered against. It's a simple extension of the golden rule. No player wants to be antagonized by his fellow players, and so he won't do it himself.

9.50 I flub an easy backhand volley to give Connors 40-15, his serve second set, but I'm ahead 4-2. After an exhausting rally I burn a forehand down the line. Then a backhand. Deuce. Connors has lost his glow. He misses a forehand approach and I outsteady him from the baseline. My game. I lead 5-2. *9.57* I double fault twice to lose the serve, letting Connors close to 3-5.

The price of Connors's intensity is fatigue. Not the type where he is huffing and puffing. More subtle. The brain is just not sending messages to his forehand as efficiently as it was earlier on. The result is obvious. *10.07* I break Jimmy for the third time in the set to square the match 3-6, 6-3.

10.12 Connors's service grunt becomes a loud hack. 30 all, 0-1, final set. He's missing his first serve frequently now. Break point. I thunder a forehand down the line but miss by an inch. Deuce. Frank Hammond, the well known chair umpire, calls the score wrong giving me the game. He makes the correction quickly adding, 'I'm sorry, I'm sorry, I'm sorry', in a descending scale so that his last apology is barely audible. A year ago the proud Hammond would never have apologized from the chair, but last September, at the US Open, he was involved in a wild melée with Ilie Nastase and John McEnroe on the Stadium Court. He was so embarrassed by being removed as umpire, that he nearly gave up officiating for good. The memory lingers. Hammond may be apologizing for the match four months ago.

10.15 Lennart smacks his lips: that dry crackling sound. *10.17* Connors asks me for confirmation that his forehand was out as called. I nod and smile. He smiles back. Despite a $100,000 purse to the winner, and the enormous pride we both have in not wanting to lose to our fiercest rival, there is still respect. *10.21* I hold to 2-1 final set. Mariana crosses her legs nervously and bites her lip at the same time. Lennart smacks again. Connors plays a loose game and I break to 3-1.

I think to myself this must be the best early round match in the game's history. In every other tournament the number one and number two meet in the finals. But in the weird world of round-robins, we could play again in the finals if both of us win our semi-finals.

10.26 I put a ball in my pocket and serve a fault, take the second out, and serve a double fault. The crowd cheers. 'I was sure it would be a fault just looking at the toss', Mariana sighs. Good serve. Deuce. Long rally from the baseline. We punish each other back and forth. In the first set, Connors had more patience. Now it's my turn. Connors hits long. My ad. Then game. 4-1.

10.30 Connors sneers at base linesman for an apparently missed call which it was not. *10.32* Bad call on my baseline, but I win the point anyway. *10.35* Ball lands an inch past my baseline – I don't even swing at ball. Linesman makes no call. 40-30 Connors. *10.37* Jimmy hits forehand I think clips back edge of line. No call. Then Hammond overrules silent baselinesman by calling ball out. Connors protests. Not so much because he wants to get this call changed, but because he might get a break on the next close one. It's the same in baseball when a player complains about being called out on a second-base tag. He just wants to get the benefit of the doubt on the next call. *10.38* Connors holds serve. 2-4.

Tennis has had an experimental rule for two years in which umpires can overrule a linesman 'if a clear mistake has been made'. The problem is that some umpires have interpreted this to mean that they should call every ball themselves, which is not the intention of the rule, and has led to chaos in many matches. As Connors said afterwards, 'not a match goes by when there is not a squabble. I'm tired of all the bull that goes on. I'm caught between my uncertainty about officials and my desire to be fair to Bjorn.'

After our match, Connors was attacked by linesman Joe Beerman, who said the verbal abuse he received from Connors was 'the worst in his twenty years in the game'.

There has been a cry for more professional, consistent officiating since open tennis began in 1968. The Eastern Tennis Umpires received $3,800 for the twenty Masters matches – each had a full complement of twelve officials. In addition there was a paid Grand Prix Supervisor on court for each match. Yet the officiating was a muddle. There is no easy answer. Some suggest that if the Eastern Umpires were paid more, they'd improve. That's crazy.

10.40 Lennart drys his hand on his trousers. Match has been running two hours. I win an endless baseline rally to lead 5-2. I'm still not tired. The points are long considering how fast the court is, but not nearly as long as the French Championships, where the slow clay courts make five-setters last five hours. The Supreme Court and the Bancroft balls used at the Garden are faster than I like. The faster the surface, the more it favours big servers like Tanner and McEnroe, and good volleyers like Gerulaitis. I would love to have more time to hit my passing shots. Lennart asked an official early in the week – very diplomatically – 'don't you think there would be more rallies on a slower surface?' He's planted the idea. Maybe next year's Masters . . .

10.45 I don't extent myself much on Connors's serve, and he quickly moves to 40-0. This is a standard strategy – one I don't always agree with – to conserve all your strength to serve out the match. One of its problems is that if you get behind on your serve, you may be angry at yourself for letting the other game go so easily. Game Connors. 3-5. Crowd yells support for Jimmy.

10.47 My serve for the match. Connors outsteadies me. 0-15. I'm still thinking how careless I was in the last point when he outlasts me again. 0-30. Damn! Why did I let the last game go so easily? I rifle a forehand uncontested down the line. 15-30. Then a backhand. 30 all. First serve fault. Long rally when Jimmy changes tactics and charges net. I'm so surprised I rush my passing shot which goes wide by a full foot. Break point. 30-40. Crowd howls. Hammond calls for quiet.

Connors punishes my serve which puts me off balance and I make another error after a short rally. Break to Connors. 4-5. Crowd shrieks as we changed ends. I've given him too many chances by not hitting hard. I'm just scared.

10.52 Connors grunts loudly and serves a fault. Some jerk high up in the green sections screams, 'double fault'. Connors's second serve just clears the net and I win the rally. 0-15. Another short rally which Connors wins on my backhand error. 15 all. These are the two shortest exchanges of the night. Maybe we both are beginning to unravel. I make another error, this time on a forehand into the net. 30-15. Connors puts a deep first serve to my backhand and I spin the ball carefully back. Then we begin to work on each other. Side to side. Short angle spinners where the service line meets the sideline, and then side to side. The best rally of the match. Finally I hit a good approach, come to net and skid a volley that lands smack on the baseline. Connors races forty feet across the court and hits a let cord drive past me. Bedlam! 40-15. I force my return. 5-all. More bedlam.

Damn. He's playing well, but how can I let him come back from 5-2? I've just been pushing the ball back. Can't play safe with Connors.

10.54 Jimmy, waiting for me to serve, is now skipping an imaginary rope like a prize-fighter after the first round. But this is the fifteenth! I hurry my second serve, and double fault. 0-15. Then a first serve fault and Connors pounces on my shallow second one. 0-30. I have heard of an athlete's wild drive late in a game called an adrenalin flush. It fits Jimmy now.

10.56 Connors spits onto the Supreme Court. I hit a low percentage drop volley to reach 15-30. Another first serve fault. But Jimmy, over anxious, hits his backhand long. 30-all. First serve fault. Now I rush my backhand which lands wide. 30-40. A break point at this stage with Connors's serve to come is considered psychologically a match point. First serve fault. God, my toss is awful. Low and in front of me instead of high and to the side. Connors just wide with a backhand. Deuce. Connors lifts his head on short forehand and pumps it into the middle of the net. My ad. Finally a good first serve. But Connors smacks a forehand return down the line that I can only stare at. Deuce. Connors hurries me with his approach and I hit into the alley. Ad Connors. It should be my match. I deserve to win. Now he has another break point. I can't believe it.

Crowd boos call as Connors drives just over the baseline. Deuce. I can't tell if the ball was good or out. It was very close. Connors comes in on deep approach and hits a savage volley winner off my pass. Ad Connors. He's impatient again with his forehand – into the net. Deuce. Connors lobs just long after we have run each other ragged. My ad. Ace. My game. 6-5 final set.

11.02 Another animal shouts 'double fault' after Connors hits his first one into the net. I whip a backhand cross-court past Jimmy at net. 0-15. He replies with a backhand down the line that I can't even reach. 15-all. I hurry my backhand, 30-15. Then a Connors forehand error. 30-all. This was definitely a tension mistake. I hadn't forced him. Long rally which I lose as my backhand hits the net and trickles into the alley. 40-30. Connors serves first one in and attacks. I attempt a pass down the line and he hits a lunge volley winner. 6-all. Tiebreak.

I ace him. 1-0. Connors hits his approach long. 2-0. We rally up and down the sidelines. I beat him twice where the ball is actually past him, but he makes a great recovery and gallops to net only just to miss a volley. Wide 3-0. He attacks the net again and swings full bore at a volley. 3-1.

11.11 Connors is now relentless. After a short exchange he charges the net and crashes a forehand volley into the corner. 3-2. Connors pays dearly for his next adventure. He comes in on a short ball which I rip past him. 4-2. Connors bounces the ball four times and faults. Another four bounces and a grunt and the second serve goes in but the approach shot doesn't. 5-2 to me. Five bounces and a fault, five bounces and a double fault. 6-2. A handful of animals cheer the double. Quadruple match point. Connors like a gored bull keeps charging. He spikes a forehand volley into the clear. 6-3. Now I serve a fault. A dozen fans applaud and another dozen hiss at their rudeness. Crowd noises are like a fugue at tournaments. One group will cheer their hero or his foe's mistakes, while the other will respond in counterpoint for their champion's deeds. Another volley winner by Connors. 6-4.

11.45 After a short rally my backhand flicks a let cord. Connors rushes in, but he's too eager and hits his backhand into the alley. Game set and match. What a way to end such a match, but I'll take it now even though I should have closed him out half an hour ago.

Later Mariana speaks to Lennart. 'I haven't watched an important match of Bjorn's for four months. I'm not used to it. I've never been so nervous. I think I'll have to train for my "watching" nerves just as much as Bjorn trains for his "playing" nerves.'

After the match, which lasted two and a half hours, I rush to the post-match press conference, where I remember two particularly dumb questions.

'Is this tournament important to you?'
'Is there something missing from your career because you've never won a tournament in New York?'

I don't remember my answers.

Record of matches between the top six players
(*until April 1980*)

World Ranking		Borg	Connors	McEnroe	Gerulaitis	Tanner	Vilas	Matches W	L	%
1	Borg	–	5	14	16	11	14	60	21	.741
2	Connors	10	–	8	15	16	4	53	25	.679
3	McEnroe	3	3	–	4	4	3	17	20	.459
4	Gerulaitis	0	2	2	–	4	3	11	41	.212
5	Tanner	4	1	4	1	–	3	13	38	.255
6	Vilas	4	4	2	5	3	–	18	27	.400

Borg's Favourite Ten Tournaments

Davis Cup (*all surfaces*)
Wimbledon (*Grass*)
US Open (*Deco Turf-Asphalt*)
French (*Clay*)
Monte Carlo (*Clay*)
Tokyo Grand Prix (*Indoors – fast surface*)
Bastaad (*Clay*)
Barcelona (*Clay*)
Montreal WCT Challenge Cup (*Indoors – fast supreme*)
Las Vegas (*Cement*)

I chose these tournaments because they are both fun to play, and important to my career. I'd rather play outdoors, in fact I prefer to do almost anything outdoors, though it's nicer when it's warm and the sun is shining. I don't like cold weather. One plays indoors because one has to, not because one wants to.

My first victory in New York, the 1980 Colgate Masters at Madison Square Garden, was a particularly sweet one (*Credit: Art Seitz*)

Bjorn Borg's Record Album

1971 and 1972	Winner of the *Orange Bowl Junior Championship*, Miami Beach, Florida
1972	Winner of *Junior Wimbledon* over Buster Mottram in finals, 6-3, 4-6, 7-5
	Davis Cup – Sweden beat New Zealand. Borg beat Parun, 4-6, 3-6, 6-3, 6-4, 6-4. Borg beat Simpson, 9-7, 6-4, 5-7, 6-1
1973	Ranks eighteen in the world
	French Open – Borg beat Richey, Barthes, Stockton, lost to Panatta
	Wimbledon – Borg beat Lall, Hombergen, Meiler, Baranyi, lost to Taylor
	US Open – Borg beat Barthes, Chanfreau, Ashe, lost to Pilic
1974	Ranks three in the world
	$266,160 in prize money
	Italian Open – Champion. Borg beat Dominguez, Pinto Bravo, Riessen, Orantes, Vilas and Nastase
	French Open – Champion. Borg beat Caujolle, Ovici, Rouyer, Van Dillen, Ramirez, Solomon and Orantes, 2-6, 6-7, 6-0, 6-1, 6-1
	Wimbledon – Borg lost to El Shafei in the third round
	US Open – Borg lost to Vijay Amritraj in the second round
1975	Ranks three in the world
	$226,851 in prize money
	French Open – Champion. Borg beat Holmes, Szoke, Hrebec, Smith, Solomon, Panatta and Vilas, 6-2, 6-3, 6-4
	Wimbledon – Borg lost in the quarter-finals to Arthur Ashe
	US Open – Borg lost to Connors in the semi-finals
	Davis Cup – Sweden wins Challenge Round first and only time.
	Sweden beat Poland, 4-1. Borg beat Drzymalski, 6-0, 6-0, 6-2. Borg beat Fibak, 6-4, 6-1, 8-6. Borg/Bengtson beat Fibak/Niedzwieski, 6-4, 6-2, 6-4.
	Sweden beat Germany, 3-2. Borg beat Meiler, 6-1, 14-12, 8-6. Borg beat Pohman, 3-6, 6-0, 6-0, 6-3
	Sweden beat Russia. Borg beat Metreveli, 7-5, 6-3, 6-3. Borg beat Volkov, 8-6, 6-1, 6-0
	Sweden beat Spain. Borg beat Higueras, 6-3, 6-1, 6-1. Borg beat Orantes, 6-4, 6-2, 6-2

Sweden beat Chile 4-1. Borg beat Cornjeo, 3-6, 6-4, 7-5, 6-3.
Borg/Bengtson beat Cornejo/Fillol, 7-5, 6-2, 3-6, 6-3. Borg beat
Fillol, 6-1, 6-2, 6-1

Sweden beat Czechoslovakia, 3-2. Borg beat Hrebec, 6-1, 6-3,
6-0. Bengtson/Borg beat Kodes/Zednick, 6-4, 6-4, 6-4. Borg
beat Kodes, 6-4, 6-1, 6-2

1976	Ranks two in the world
	$424,420 in prize money

WCT Dallas Final – Borg beat Dibbs, Solomon and Vilas,
1-6, 6-1, 7-5

French Open – Borg lost to Panatta in the quarter-finals, 3-6,
3-6, 6-2, 6-7

Wimbledon – Champion. Borg beat D. Lloyd, Riessen, Dibley,
Gottfried, Vilas, Tanner, and Nastase, 6-4, 6-2, 9-7

US Open – Borg beaten by Connors in finals, 4-6, 6-3, 6-7,
4-6

1977	Ranks two in the world
	$337,020 in prize money

Wimbledon – Champion. Borg beat Zugarelli, Edmonson, Pilic,
Fibak, Nastase, Gerulaitis and Connors, 3-6, 6-2, 6-1, 5-7, 6-4.

US Open – Borg defaulted to Stockton in fourth round

1978	Ranks three in the world
	$691,886 in prize money

Wimbledon – Champion. Borg beat Amaya, McNamara, Fillol,
Masters, S. Mayer, Okker, and Connors, 6-2, 6-2, 6-3.

US Open – Borg beat Hewitt, Gunthardt, Mitton, Solomon,
Ramirez, Gerulaitis, lost to Connors, 4-6, 2-6, 2-6

French Open – Champion. Borg beat Deblicker, Fagel,
Bertolucci, Tanner, Ramirez, Barazutti, and Vilas, 6-1, 6-1, 6-3

1979	Ranks one in the world
	$1,019,345 in prize money

French Open – Champion. Borg beat Pecci, 6-3, 6-1, 6-7, 6-4

Wimbledon – Champion. Borg beat Gorman, Amritraj, Pfister,
Teacher, Okker, Connors, and Tanner, 6-7, 7-1, 3-6, 6-3, 6-4

1980	As of 1 July ranks one in the world

Colgate Grand Prix Masters – Champion. Borg beat Tanner,
Connors, Higueras, McEnroe, and Gerulaitis, 7-5, 6-2

10. Finishing strokes

Tennis has become so popular so fast that its explosive growth is out of control most of the time. There seems to be no direction to the development of the sport – unless it is every direction at once.

A continual tug of war rages over who has the most influence in tennis. For almost a hundred years, the game was totally controlled by amateur associations in each country, linked together by an austere world body called the International Tennis Federation. They had ultimate power over rules, players, the Davis Cup, tournaments – everything, in fact. The players had no rights whatsoever. For example, before 1968 (the first year of open tennis), American amateurs were required to return to the US for their country's circuit immediately after Wimbledon. They had no choice. Furthermore, Americans could only compete outside the US for six weeks a year. And until 1973, European players had to join their nation's Davis Cup team or risk suspension.

Certainly, the out of date thinking of the ITF and its member nations retarded the natural growth of tennis. For instance, there was a time when the ITF considered a man's turning professional the same as his turning gangster. Though what took the place of the ITF's power was not all good either.

With the advent of open tennis and the ATP (players' union), the balance of power has swung dramatically in the players' favour. In addition, US anti-trust laws have reduced the powers of the US Tennis Association, which once regulated the dates and the number of tournaments with an iron hand, to minor administrative ones.

The ATP did a remarkable job of running the game democratically. Before open tennis, players often got into tournaments by being a friend of the local director or a good 'after dinner' speaker. There was no selection for entry on merit until the ATP developed the first computerized world ranking system in 1974. Prize money was increased, generous sponsorship was encouraged and dozens of new tournaments sprang up around the world.

There are lots of things to do outdoors, but let others do the jogging and running (opposite) (*Credit: E.L. Scott*)

The ATP initiated two programmes to regulate and improve officiating. One of half a dozen 'supervisors' oversees every single grand prix tournament to ensure that rules are enforced uniformly around the world. In addition, the ATP runs a school for officials in Dallas and Europe once a year to train linespersons in their sometimes controversial skills. Also, the ATP has established a code of conduct for players, with appropriate fines and suspensions for misbehaviour. The supervisors, officials' school, and code of conduct are far from perfect, but they are a step towards correcting the game's deficiences.

I have not always been an enthusiastic supporter of the ATP because, for a long time, it was controlled by Donald Dell, Bob Briner, and Jack Kramer, who did not always have my best interests at heart. Dell is the lawyer/agent for over fifty pros, as well as a promoter for many tournaments, and the most powerful man in tennis. For years, he was also the lawyer for the ATP and he still controls the ATP's television interests. He does not represent me, and I felt that he might naturally favour his clients over me. This may be human nature, but I don't think it is fair, therefore, for him to be so close to the ATP. Briner was Executive Director of the ATP for five years and he was too close to Dell for my comfort. Kramer has criticized Jimmy Connors and me in the press for being selfish and not playing enough tournaments, and then he wonders why I won't play in his tournaments! Kramer was the first Executive Director of the ATP but has switched roles from 'labour' to 'management' and is now the tournament directors' North American representative to the Men's Pro Council, which has run the professional game for three years.

The Council is taking positive steps to clear the chaos in the tennis jungle. It is formed of nine men, three representatives from each of the players, the tournaments, and the ITF, and is headed by a Frenchman Philippe Chatrier, who is also President of his own French Association and of the ITF. Chatrier is strong and fair, which is not to say I agree with him all the time. I don't. Chatrier thinks Connors, Vilas, McEnroe, Gerulaitis and myself play too many 'big money' exhibitions and damage the success of tournaments, but he's wrong. Most of our exhibitions are in cities that can't have grand prix tournaments, or don't want them because they can't be certain that top players will play.

So the Council is always trying to devise rules to limit the number of exhibitions we can play. But if I didn't play exhibitions (and I only play them four weeks of the year when I'm permitted to play six), they are wrong in assuming that I'd play more tournaments instead. I wouldn't. I'd go home to Monte Carlo and rest.

My winning four Wimbledons and four French Opens, and Connors's winning the Open three times, grants us a privilege that is worth more than the difference between the winner's purse and the runner-up's prize. It is our good fortune to be in demand as giant gate attractions for one- or two-night exhibitions. In a tournament the public isn't guaranteed we'll play against each other, and the crowd has to wait a week until the Sunday finals, if then, to see us play together. Either of us could lose before then. Whereas the promoter of an exhibition will pay us a handsome fee simply for our appearance against each other. Anyone who says we should give up this incredible opportunity is crazy.

This opportunity is only available to the top three or four players in the world, and we have worked harder and longer than anyone else to get to the top. The suggestion that we should refuse to play exhibitions 'for the good of the game' is usually put forward by someone who runs a tournament we won't play in.

But there are two areas of tennis that are sadly backward. The first is player conduct. The rude gestures and language that have become a standard part of our game are unbelieveable. What's the answer? The solution is not, as some believe, to fine the top players very heavily. They make too much money and any fine would be treated merely as a business expense. Suspensions would hurt the game even more, because the offenders would be unavailable for tournaments already desperate for as many of the best top names as possible. If you banned Connors for two months, he'd simply go to South America for an exhibition tour and make more than he could on the Grand Prix circuit.

I don't mean this to condemn my friends Connors, McEnroe, or Nastase either. Their behaviour is a result of the total lack of discipline or of enforcement procedures in tennis. Further fuelling their anger is the fact that there is no improvement in the poor standards of line calling, which result in players complaining about *good* calls that go against them because linesmen have been mistaken so often in the past.

The cure for poor sportsmanship is drastic but simple. As you know, my own temper was cooled forever by my being suspended for almost half a year when I was young! We should forget about today's adult tennis pros and work on the younger generation. How? The next time a twelve-year-old tosses his racket or swears, kick him out of the game for four months. There would be some irate parents for a while, and maybe a few law suits, but if the national associations stuck together, the sorry disease of tennis tantrums could be cured very quickly!

The second major worry is the lack of planning for the future of tennis. The game has never been more prosperous but no one – the ATP, the ITF, national associations, sponsors, or private promoters – has budgeted a penny for training future stars. There should be dozens of international training grounds for juniors. And there should be testing sites for equipment and devices that would improve our sport. For instance, more research funds to develop the electronic line calling device I mentioned. Also, the machinery for changing rules is creaky and obsolete. For example, in 1975, there were four tiebreak formulae in use, all officially accepted. Wimbledon's tiebreak started when the games were at 8-all, the other three at 6-all. These included the US Open's 12-point tiebreak, Newport's 9-point 'sudden death', and WCT's 13-point. Our game looked foolish with so many scoring systems. Another thing. How can the ITF ban 'spaghetti stringing' and yet not ban the Prince oversize racket? For over a hundred years, tennis has been alone in not having any restrictions on the size or shape of its equipment. A racket could be ten feet long and made of titanium. The only fixed standard is that it must be conventionally strung. The inconsistency is obvious. Either you permit any sort of racket, or you specifically detail size, shape, and material, just as golf does with golf clubs.

The most often heard solution for the game's problems is the appointment of an international commissioner. The suggestion is naïve. Tennis is so fragmented that no one would give up his own area of control. Open tennis started in 1968 without any structure. In the absence of any organization, a dozen lawyers, agents, officials, promoters and sponsors jumped in to grab a piece of the cake, just as a century ago American homesteaders rushed in to mark off their small parcel of land.

Some of the chaos in tennis has been healthy, in that new ideas have not been slowed down by the sort of old fashioned thinking that stifles the Olympics, for example. The price of our sport's crazy growth might sometimes have been total disorder, but one day the dust will settle – and without a commissioner. In the meantime, the paying and playing public should ignore our game's occasional predicaments and just go out and hit a few. That's what I'm going to do.

Index